Archives

IN SEARCH OF MEDIA

Götz Bachmann, Timon Beyes, Mercedes Bunz, and Wendy Hui Kyong Chun, Series Editors

Archives

**Andrew Lison, Marcell Mars,
Tomislav Medak, and Rick Prelinger**

IN SEARCH OF MEDIA

University of Minnesota Press
Minneapolis
London

meson press

In Search of Media is a collaboration between the University
of Minnesota Press and meson press, an open access
publisher, https://meson.press.

Published by the
University of Minnesota Press, 2019
111 Third Avenue South, Suite 290
Minneapolis, MN 55401-2520
https://www.upress.umn.edu

in collaboration with
meson press
Salzstrasse 1
21335 Lüneburg, Germany
https://meson.press

ISBN 978-1-5179-0806-5 (pb)
A Cataloging-in-Publication record for this book is available
from the Library of Congress.

UMP BmB

Contents

Series Foreword

"Media determine our situation," Friedrich Kittler infamously wrote in his Introduction to *Gramophone, Film, Typewriter.* Although this dictum is certainly extreme—and media archaeology has been critiqued for being overly dramatic and focused on technological developments—it propels us to keep thinking about media as setting the terms for which we live, socialize, communicate, organize, do scholarship, et cetera. After all, as Kittler continued in his opening statement almost thirty years ago, our situation, "in spite or because" of media, "deserves a description." What, then, are the terms—the limits, the conditions, the periods, the relations, the phrases—of media? And, what is the relationship between these terms and determination? This book series, *In Search of Media,* answers these questions by investigating the often elliptical "terms of media" under which users operate. That is, rather than produce a series of explanatory keyword-based texts to describe media practices, the goal is to understand the conditions (the "terms") under which media is produced, as well as the ways in which media impacts and changes these terms.

Clearly, the rise of search engines has fostered the proliferation and predominance of keywords and terms. At the same time, it has changed the very nature of keywords, since now any word and pattern can become "key." Even further, it has transformed the very process of learning, since search presumes that, (a) with the right phrase, any question can be answered and (b) that the answers lie within the database. The truth, in other words, is "in there." The impact of search/media on knowledge, however, goes beyond search engines. Increasingly, disciplines—from sociology to economics, from the arts to literature—are in search of media as a way to revitalize their methods and objects of study. Our current media situation therefore seems to imply a new term, understood as temporal shifts of mediatic conditioning. Most broadly, then, this series asks: What are the terms or conditions of knowledge itself?

To answer this question, each book features interventions by two (or more) authors, whose approach to a term—to begin with: *communication, pattern discrimination, markets, remain, machine, archives*—diverge and converge in surprising ways. By pairing up scholars from North America and Europe, this series also advances media theory by obviating the proverbial "ten year gap" that exists across language barriers due to the vagaries of translation and local academic customs. The series aims to provoke new descriptions, prescriptions, and hypotheses—to rethink and reimagine what media can and must do.

Introduction

Contesting "The Archive," Archives, and Thanatarchy

Andrew Lison

The questions of search that animate this series cannot be adequately answered without also considering the issue of retrieval, nor can the question of the acquisition of knowledge be addressed without attending to the subject of its availability. Although so much of our day-to-day experience of twenty-first-century life seems conditioned by a continuous and often overwhelming virtual flow of information, scholars have long emphasized the material and infrastructural factors that enable such a state of affairs (e.g., Hayles 1999; Starosielski 2015; Hu 2015; Parks and Starosielski 2015). The authors in this volume make a similar contribution to our understanding of archives in an age in which near-instant access to information can encourage us to take these repositories of informational, mediatic, and physical artifacts for granted. Situated at the intersection of the material and immaterial, the institutional and the independent, and, most importantly, the theoretical and the practical, the essays collected here challenge our conception of archives as either transparent conduits for storage and retrieval or sites of hierarchical, top-down dissemination. In short, they contest both the philosophy of "the archive" and the implementation of really-existing archives as they have been heretofore conceived. In this spirit, this introduction seeks not only to offer context for their interventions but make some of its own.

The central relationship of curated resources to research within academic disciplines has meant that archival practice and scholarship have long existed in a relationship of complex symbiosis. On the scholarly side, theoretical considerations of the archive have steadily gained currency within the academy since the end of the Second World War and, not coincidentally, the rise of digital technologies. Many thinkers (e.g., Huhtamo and Parikka 2011, 6–7; Foster et al. 2016, 319–23[1]) connect these developments to the earlier rise of photography and its decentering effects both as analyzed by Walter Benjamin (Benjamin 1969a) and specifically taken up in relation to archives by André Malraux, whose essay "Museum without Walls," published shortly after the end of the war, noted that "an earlier generation thrived on Michelangelo; now we are given photographs of lesser masters, likewise of folk paintings and arts hitherto ignored . . . For while photography is bringing a profusion of masterpieces to the artists, these latter have been revising their notion of what it is that makes the masterpiece" (Malraux 1978, 17). Michel Foucault's reconsideration of the conditions of knowledge production over the 1960s and 1970s, which led him to declare that "in that area where, in the past, history deciphered the traces left by men, it now deploys a mass of elements that have to be grouped, made relevant, placed in relation to one another to form totalities" (Foucault 2010, 7), is a high-water mark of poststructuralist intervention into archival theory, delineating precisely the kind of work that he would label archaeology. His *Archaeology of Knowledge* thus offers a historically and archivally centered complement to the broader, information-theory-inflected analyses of language, subjectivity, and culture put forth by his contemporaries in France.[2] Subsequently, artist-theorist Allan Sekula would make his own intervention into the conceptualization of the archive, examining how not only photography but the statistical documentation and pseudoscientific analysis of bodily features were crucial to the establishment of nineteenth-century archives of population control and management in order to argue that "every proper portrait has its lurking, objectifying inverse in the files of the police" (Sekula 1986, 7).

The eruption of digital media into the popular consciousness beginning in the late 1980s and early 1990s and reaching a fever pitch with the mainstream adoption of the Internet a few years later has effected a reconsideration of these earlier treatments in light of the vast global changes in the production, storage, and consumption of knowledge precipitated by this technological shift. Although precedents exist, particularly in cinema studies, the paradiscipline of media archaeology, which examines the historical development of media technologies, especially through unrealized directions or prototypical stages from which they could have proceeded but did not, has risen in parallel with the homogenizing effect of this digital turn.[3] This attention to the specificities of archaic media technologies and formats results, at least in part, from the way that computation renders previously distinct media forms and technologies equivalent via binary encoding and accessible through global networks of on-demand transmission and reception. In the mid-1980s, these imminent developments led one of the most preeminent forerunners of media archaeology, Friedrich Kittler—himself intimately familiar with the connections between poststructuralist thought and digital technologies—to remark of Foucault that "even writing itself, before it ends up in libraries, is a communication medium, the technology of which the archaeologist simply forgot. It is for this reason that all his analyses end immediately before that point in time at which other media penetrated the library's stacks. Discourse analysis cannot be applied to sound archives or towers of film rolls" (Kittler 1999, 5). Kittler's own reconsideration of these three mediatic forms in anticipation of their collapse into the multimedia PC would be followed by the ruminations of another poststructuralist philosopher, Jacques Derrida, on the cultural significance of telecommunications, and electronic mail in particular, in a 1994 lecture subsequently published in English under the title *Archive Fever*. There, he argued that "the technical structure of the *archiving* archive also determines the structure of the *archivable* content even in its very coming into existence and in its relationship to the future" (Derrida 1996, 17). Such a conception of the technological conditioning of archives is pushed to a point of inversion by media archaeologist Wolfgang Ernst, who has suggested that the ostensibly universal structuration that digitally networked multimedia represents results in "an anarchive of sensory data for which no genuine archival culture has been developed so far in the occident" (Ernst 2013, 139; see also Reynolds 2011b, 27).

These shifts in the scholarly approach to archives have at times anticipated, and at others responded to, changes in archival practice itself. As the notion of archives and archivable materials has expanded, there has been a corresponding emphasis on acknowledging the perspectives of archivists and the labor of archiving itself. The digital humanities has been a key driver of this shift. For example, in reflecting on her work at the Women Writers Project, Julia Flanders reminds us that "for every hour of scholarly research in an office or library, countless other hours are spent building and maintaining the vast research apparatus of books, databases, libraries, servers, networks, cataloguing and metadata standards, thesauri, and systems of access" (Flanders 2012, 306). As noted by Rick Prelinger in this volume, this frequently overlooked work is often disproportionately undertaken by women and/or people of color, a fact emphasized by analyses like Leah Henrickson's consideration of hands inadvertently captured performing the labor of scanning books for Google's searchable archive of the printed word (Henrickson 2014), even while the results of automated search queries themselves are often biased against these very same subject positions (Olofsson 2015; Noble 2018). In this sense, appeals such as Miriam Posner's for "ripping apart and rebuilding the machinery of the archive and database so that it does not reproduce the logic that got us here in the first place" (Posner 2016, 35) can be understood as doing for the software routines and metadata schemas of digital curation what media-archaeological approaches have promised to do for hardware.[4]

More recently, scholars and archivists alike, not to mention those occupying the increasing number of syntheses between these roles, have arrived at a shared understanding that has, in truth, been with us the entire time, namely that "immaterial," digital and material, physical media alike remain of archival interest—a realization following what Florian Cramer has more generally described as "the post-digital condition" (Cramer 2014)—and, as such, demand accounting for in both their particularity and generality. It is under these circumstances that the authors in this volume, as both practitioners and theorists of archives both digital and analog, offer their contributions, for the current state of affairs has also effected if not a reconciliation between then at least an amalgam of archival theory and praxis. The three other contributors to this volume all have experience curating and administering archives as well as in thinking through the implications of these practices, as do I, to a lesser extent, as a former systems administrator, student employee of my undergraduate institution's library, and volunteer working for many years in and alongside its radio station's music library, and presently as a media scholar. Moreover, many of the archives in question, from the library Prelinger runs together with his partner Megan, the Internet Archive on whose board he sits, and the Prelinger Archives whose audiovisual holdings he curates to the free online Public Library administered by Marcell Mars and Tomislav Medak at https://www.memoryoftheworld.org/, and even the college radio library, exist outside of, if not in opposition to, official structures for the accumulation, organization, and preservation of knowledge.

The Prelinger Library, for example, routinely takes in materials that other archives have either discarded or would never consider in the first place, while Public Library, as Mars noted in the keynote panel to the second Terms of Media conference, at Brown University, that forms the basis for this collection, has crucially preserved books from the former Yugoslavia that were purged from Croatian holdings in the wake of the collapse of state socialism in the early 1990s and the region's subsequent ethnic warfare.[5] Even the KALX library contains key recordings documenting of the rise of punk rock, hip-hop, and electronic music in the San Francisco Bay Area and the anti-apartheid movement of the 1980s (to offer just two examples) that the University of California at Berkeley's music library has seemingly been content to overlook, albeit perhaps to the satisfaction of those who curate it (see Levine 2014). These unconventional archives, in other words, contest the status of an institutional archival practice that has often been relegated to playing catch-up in the wake of the Internet's popularization of search and retrieval even more than they do the prognostications of supposedly unpracticed theoreticians. If Google's absorption of the majority of the world's informational queries represents a totalizing expansion of knowledge retrieval under the privatizing conditions of neoliberalism, then unconventional archives contest this dominance by privileging a more eccentric curatorial touch.

These expanded archival practices can become contentious when they run up against the norms and structures erected to underwrite the dissemination of knowledge in the era of physical media—that is, in the age of the printed book, newspaper, magazine, and journal. Since the notion of informational ownership in the digital age essentially comes down to the ability to assert control over a stream of ones and zeroes (see, e.g., Kittler 1992, 85–6) within what is now a globally networked sphere of discursive production, this poses a threat to an older model that, as Mars and Medak argue, is built upon the governmental granting of corporate printing rights in early modern Europe. Their chapter therefore examines the implications of copyright law in relation to their Public Library project, which is situated here in opposition to a corporatized academic publishing industry dependent on unremunerated scholarly labor for its enviable profits. Charting the history of copyright in Western society through its inception to the present moment, they identify our current situation as a critical conjuncture for digital media, one in which tendencies toward the open exchange of information and the amalgamation of scholarly knowledge behind proprietary portals are at loggerheads. Building

on the theories of Gilles Deleuze and Félix Guattari, they argue that
the extreme privatization of academic productivity by scholarly
publishing conglomerates, combined with the ongoing proletari-
anization of the professoriate, who are often obliged to write and
edit without payment from precarious positions within and outside
the academy simply for a chance at landing secure employment,
have led to what they call "a schizoid impasse sustained by a failed
metaphor": intellectual property. Public Library's choice to offer
academic works regardless of these considerations, they argue,
expanding upon the philosophy of the late information activist
Aaron Swartz, who took his own life amidst a legal battle resulting
from his efforts to download a vast range of papers from scholarly
publishing clearinghouse JSTOR, is a political act that stands in
opposition to an exploitative and increasingly archaic legal regime,
offering another way forward for the preservation and dissemination of knowledge.

Prelinger's essay, on the other hand, examines the contemporary
status of archives as material and theoretical constructs, the
tensions between these two facets that run through them, and
the contradictory, utopian possibilities that they can offer. Part
scholarly analysis, part professional anecdote, and part extension
of the conversations between archivists that circulate around the
clock with lightning speed via social media, Prelinger formulates
a theory and practice of archives—in explicit opposition to that
of "the archive"—that paradoxically situates their future(s) in the
inconveniences they present. From the labor of archivists to the potentially hazardous materials that form the support for "old media,"
these disruptions in the smooth storage and retrieval of information, materials, and media form the backdrop against which the
continuing production and reproduction of knowledge takes place.
Archives become loci of debate, where, as with media archaeology,
the past is kept, revisited, and reformulated with an eye toward
as-yet-unimaginable futures. For Prelinger, the Internet amplifies
and extends this process, but should not do so at the expense
of physical artifacts, which are at risk, he argues, of something

"akin to urban gentrification" by the nonpresence of immaterial records. We can thus consider physical media themselves, and not simply in their more dangerous forms like nitrate film, as a kind of inconvenience for which archives are well suited. Yet he also argues that archives cannot become totalities—that they will have to deal with loss, as the historical record has in fact always done, but which, in our contemporary moment of supposedly seamless digital reproducibility, seems somehow unthinkably traumatic. They will also have to negotiate the fine line between preservation and surveillance as, for example, records and holdings in the era of pervasive metadata may reveal much more about their creators and users than they have in the past, as well as the relationships between amateur and professional archivists and institutional and noninstitutional archives in a society where, via the decreasing cost of digital storage capacity, archives, or "archives," are made almost by default.[6] It is ultimately difficulties like these, however, that, for Prelinger, enable archives as sites of contestation and possibility, and for which they must be preserved against the precarity-inducing drive toward convenience.

These essays reimagine the potentiality of archives at a time when institutional support for preserving physical collections is hard won and corporate interests are rapidly consolidating their control over the digital distribution of knowledge, situating them in opposition to these unsettling trends. Yet I want to conclude this overview with a broader provocation: what if archives themselves, and the focus on the past they necessarily embody, either cannot or can no longer be the staging grounds for the future that media archae-ologists and archivists so often insist that they are? If Benjamin's writing on photography is a point of departure for many postwar reflections on the changing nature of the archive, then it is a senti-ment expressed in one of the last essays he ever wrote that forms the backdrop to much of the more recent emphasis on media archaeology, the archive, and archives alike: "The past carries with it a temporal index by which it is referred to redemption . . . Every image of the past that is not recognized by the present as one of its own concerns threatens to disappear irretrievably" (Benjamin 1969b, 254–5).[7] At our particular point in history, however, as the social significance of archives is continually championed, knowledge becomes increasingly digitized and accessible, analog media experience a resurgence of popular and intellectual interest, and mining rhetorical opponents' social media feeds for compromising previous statements has become a staple of online argumentation, we are more likely to experience the past as inescapable and even damning than as precarious and latently redemptive. Under such circumstances, does it still make sense to valorize the omnivorous preservation of the past? Or should we perhaps instead counterpoise to Benjamin's Marxism, which led him to declare that "only that historian will have the gift of fanning the spark of hope in the past who is firmly convinced that *even the dead* will not be safe from the enemy if he wins" (Benjamin 1969b, 255), Marx's own well-known statement that "the tradition of all the dead generations weighs like a nightmare on the brain of the living" (Marx 1963, 15)?

The introduction of Marxism into the question of archives is not arbitrary, for it is precisely at the intersection of these two modes of thought that some of the most penetrating analysis of recent years has been located. This critique has risen in large part out of popular music writing associated with the blogosphere, which is to say a sector that is intimately familiar with both unconventional archives—given that popular music, even at its most obscure, aesthetically innovative, and/or theoretical, has rarely been welcomed into institutional collections with the same vigor as books or even films—and the potentialities that the Internet can offer for the storage, retrieval, dissemination, and discussion of underrepresented media artifacts. It is thus all the more surprising, then, that it should be one that expresses exasperation with the conditions of stagnation that seem to accompany the increasing tendency toward archival totalization. The recently departed and already sorely missed Mark Fisher's *Capitalist Realism,* for example, which analyzes the sociocultural effects of neoliberalism since the collapse of state-socialist alternatives to capitalism in the late

1980s and early 1990s, begins with a reading of Alfonso Cuarón's cinematic adaptation of P. D. James's novel *The Children of Men,* in which "cultural treasures—Michelangelo's *David,* Picasso's *Guernica,* Pink Floyd's inflatable pig—are preserved in a building that is itself a refurbished heritage artifact . . . our only glimpse into the lives of the elite, holed up against the effects of a catastrophe which has caused mass sterility" (Fisher 2009, 1). While Fisher himself blogged under the name K-Punk, music critic and prolific blogger Simon Reynolds has also taken up this critique in his book *Retromania* to more explicitly examine the state of popular music in the twenty-first century thus far, made and experienced under conditions of previously inconceivable access to the styles of the past, writing that "the very people who you would once have expected to produce (as artists) or champion (as consumers) the non-traditional and the groundbreaking . . . they've switched roles to become curators and archivists. The avant-garde is now an arrière-garde" (Reynolds 2011b, xix–xx). These considerations draw upon earlier Marxist analyses, most notably those of Fredric Jameson and particularly his study of the pastiche-laden aesthetics of postmodernism (Jameson 1991), as well as the connection drawn by Derrida between what he calls "*le mal d'archive,* archive fever" and the recapitulatory urge of the psychoanalytic death drive, or Thanatos (Derrida 1996, 12; see also Reynolds 2011b, 26–8). While this skepticism of the drive to archive is gaining increasing purchase within the academy,[8] it is notable that it is at the intersection of theoretically informed, crate-digging music writers and digital file-sharing networks that the preservationist impulse embodied in archives has birthed its most trenchant critics.

If the status of music collections as archives frequently curated outside of official spaces and organized by an intensely personal sense of significance has led some who collect and write about music to reflect upon the exhaustion of that significance post-Napster, however, their observations are of great import for any theory or practice of archives as they are more generally construed today. As Fisher writes,

> We do not need to wait for *Children of Men*'s near-future
> to arrive to see this transformation of culture into muse-
> um pieces. The power of capitalist realism derives in part
> from the way that capitalism subsumes and consumes
> all of previous history: one effect of its "system of equiva-
> lence" which can assign all cultural objects . . . a monetary
> value. (Fisher 2009, 4)

Capitalism is far from the only system of general equivalence,
but the Marxist analysis of the money form may represent the
ur-model for understanding them more broadly:[9] both the digital,
in which all expressions are reduced to binary alternations, and
the archive operate under similar principles.[10] As Sekula notes of
nineteenth-century attempts to establish a physiological typology
of criminal tendencies, "it was only on the basis of mutual compari-
son, on the basis of the tentative construction of a larger, 'universal'
archive, that zones of deviance and respectability could be clearly
demarcated" (Sekula 1986, 14), yet this determining structural influence might not be the only effect of what he calls "the fundamental
problem of the archive, the problem of volume" (29). In his publici-
zation of information theorist Claude Shannon's seminal paper on
communication as a mathematical problem, Warren Weaver wrote
that, as the transformation of messages irrespective of medium
into discrete, statistically determinable units for which they both
considered binary encoding exemplary, "one has the vague feeling
that information and meaning may prove to be something like a
pair of canonically conjugate variables in quantum theory, they
being subject to some joint restriction that condemns a person to
the sacrifice of the one as he insists on having much of the other"
(Weaver 1998, 28).[11] This suspicion lurks behind much of Reynolds's
thinking in *Retromania,* as when he writes that "it's easy to imagine
that as the collection's size approaches infinity, the appetite to listen to music shrinks to infinitesimal" (Reynolds 2011b, 111). Whether within a realm of intellectual-property-free digital transmission
or the inconvenient utopias of unorthodoxically curated physical
spaces, archivists, scholars, and theorists will have to address the

suffocating effect of stockpiled history, and not just the breadth and organization of its collected artifacts, if archives are to remain much-needed sites of contestation against the current wave of global reaction, which threatens to erase the past not in order to move forward, but to repeat its abominations anew.

Notes

1   This section cited, written by Rosalind Krauss, focuses on the historical signif-icance of Benjamin and Malraux, but see also Hal Foster's analysis of archival tendencies in contemporary art in Foster et al., 782–3.

2   For more on this latter set of developments, see Lison 2014.

3   See Huhtamo and Parikka 2011. Jussi Parikka, in an excellent and accessible introduction to the field, enumerates as precursors in film studies the propo-nents of so-called apparatus theory, Christian Metz, Jean-Louis Baudry, and Jean-Louis Comolli (key texts of whose are collected in Rosen 1986) alongside feminist film scholar Laura Mulvey (Mulvey 1975) and "the by-now classic 34th International Federation of Film Archives—FIAF, www.fiafnet.org—conference in Brighton in 1978" (Parikka 2012, 9).

4   Indeed, one of the most thought-provoking efforts to articulate the methods of the digital humanities and media archaeology together also lies, perhaps unsurprisingly, at the intersection of software and hardware in the attempt to develop media theorist Kara Keeling's concept of a queer operating system (Keeling 2014) into a set of technical specificities (Barnett et al. 2016).

5   Mars and Prelinger's talks can be viewed together at https://www.youtube.com/watch?v=kvzuUgP6d3Q; the collection in question can be accessed at https://otpisane.memoryoftheworld.org/.

6   For more on this development see, e.g., Reynolds 2011b, discussed further below.

7   It is presumably due to views like these that Erkki Huhtamo and Parikka describe Benjamin as "arguably the most prominent forerunner—beside Foucault—of media-archaeological modes of cultural analysis" (Huhtamo and Parikka 2011, 6). Simon Reynolds has similarly written that "Benjamin and Borges are the avatars of our 'time out of joint' era" (Reynolds 2011a, 34).

8   See, for example, literary and theatre scholar Emma Smith's talk at The Ox-ford Research Centre in the Humanities 2016 colloquium "What Does It Mean to Be Human in the Digital Age?", viewable at https://www.youtube.com/watch?v=Eq51l1XyDmQ.

9   Although he does not go quite this far, on this theme see Parikka 2012, 36–7. Readers will also be interested in Jens Schröter's talk at the first Terms of Media conference, in Lüneburg, Germany, entitled "Money Determines Our Situation" and viewable at https://vimeo.com/133636177, as well as the written version

published as part of the corresponding volume in the present series (Beverungen et al. 2019). Since in Marxism, arguably more than anywhere else, time is money, Flanders's consideration of the corporatized academy's insistence on the general equivalency of project time for nonfaculty work (which would of course include archival labor) is also relevant (Flanders 2012, 303–6).

10   On this latter point, see Sekula's conception of the photographic archive as "a relation of general equivalence between images," which, in its "capacity . . . to reduce all possible sights to a single code of equivalence was grounded . . . in the universal abstract language of mathematics" and measurement (Sekula 1986, 17), in advance of "an operationalist model of knowledge, based on the 'general equivalence' established by the numerical shorthand code" (57). It is of course now difficult in retrospect not to understand this shorthand as a forerunner to binary, digital encoding, especially since Sekula himself even connects it with the contemporaneous technology of the telegraph (33). See also Krauss's observations on photography more widely, building on Benjamin and Malraux, in Foster et al. 2016, 320–2, as well as Parikka 2012, 37 on all of the above.

11   For more on this development and its broader implications, see Hayles 1999, Terranova 2004, 6–38, and Lison 2014.

References

Barnett, Fiona, Zach Blas, micha cárdenas, Jacob Gaboury, Jessica Marie Johnson, and Margaret Rhee. 2016. "QueerOS: A User's Manual." In *Debates in the Digital Humanities 2016,* eds. Matthew K. Gold and Lauren F. Klein, 50–9. Minneapolis: University of Minnesota Press.

Benjamin, Walter. 1969a. "The Work of Art in the Age of Mechanical Reproduction" (1936). In Walter Benjamin, *Illuminations,* ed. Hannah Arendt, trans. Harry Zohn, 217–51. New York: Schocken.

Benjamin, Walter. 1969b. "Theses on the Philosophy of History" (1940). In Walter Benjamin, *Illuminations,* ed. Hannah Arendt, trans. Harry Zohn, 253–64. New York: Schocken.

Beverungen, Armin, Philip Mirowski, Edward Nik-Khah, and Jens Schröter. 2019. *Markets.* Lüneburg, Germany, and Minneapolis: meson press and University of Minnesota Press.

Cramer, Florian. 2014. "What Is 'Post-digital'?" *APRJA* 3, no. 1. Accessed April 29, 2019. https://www.aprja.net/what-is-post-digital/.

Derrida, Jacques. 1996. *Archive Fever: A Freudian Impression* (1994/1995). Trans. Eric Prenowitz. Chicago: University of Chicago Press.

Ernst, Wolfgang. 2013. "Discontinuities: Does the Archive Become Metaphorical in Multimedia Space?" (2006). In Wolfgang Ernst, *Digital Memory and the Archive,* ed. Jussi Parikka, 113–40. Minneapolis: University of Minnesota Press.

Fisher, Mark. 2009. *Capitalist Realism: Is There No Alternative?* Winchester, U.K.: Zero Books.

Flanders, Julia. 2012. "Time, Labor, and 'Alternate Careers' in Digital Humanities Knowledge Work" (2011). In *Debates in the Digital Humanities,* ed. Matthew K. Gold, 292–308. Minneapolis: University of Minnesota Press.

Foster, Hal, Rosalind Krauss, Yve-Alain Bois, Benjamin H. D. Buchloh, and David Joselit. 2016. *Art Since 1900* (2004), 3rd edition. London: Thames & Hudson.

Foucault, Michel. 2010. *The Archaeology of Knowledge and the Discourse on Language* (1969/1971). Trans. A. M. Sheridan Smith (1972). New York: Vintage Books.

Hayles, N. Katherine. 1999. *How We Became Posthuman: Virtual Bodies in Cybernetics, Literature, and Informatics.* Chicago: University of Chicago Press.

Henrickson, Leah. 2014. "The Darker Side of Digitization." Blog. Accessed June 29, 2018. https://bhilluminated.wordpress.com/2014/03/20/google-book-scanners/.

Hu, Tung-Hui. 2015. *A Prehistory of the Cloud.* Cambridge, Mass.: MIT Press.

Huhtamo, Erkki, and Jussi Parikka. 2011. "Introduction: An Archaeology of Media Archaeology." In *Media Archaeology: Approaches, Applications, and Implications,* eds. Erkki Huhtamo and Jussi Parikka, 1–21. Berkeley: University of California Press.

Jameson, Fredric. 1991. *Postmodernism, or The Cultural Logic of Late Capitalism.* Durham, N.C.: Duke University Press.

Keeling, Kara. 2014. "Queer OS." *Cinema Journal* 53, no. 2 (Winter): 152–7.

Kittler, Friedrich. 1992. "There Is No Software." *Stanford Literature Review* 9, no. 1 (Spring): 81–90.

Kittler, Friedrich A. 1999. *Gramophone, Film, Typewriter* (1986). Trans. Geoffrey Winthrop-Young and Michael Wutz. Stanford, Calif.: Stanford University Press.

Levine, Kendra K. 2014. "When a College Takes the Music Library of a College Radio Station." *Library Attack* blog. Accessed April 29, 2019. https://libraryattack.com/when-a-college-takes-the-music-library-of-a-college-radio-station/.

Lison, Andrew. 2014. "1968 and the Future of Information." In *The Global Sixties in Sound and Vision: Media, Counterculture, Revolt,* eds. Timothy Scott Brown and Andrew Lison, 245–74. Basingstoke, U.K.: Palgrave Macmillan.

Malraux, André. 1978. "Museum without Walls" (1947). In André Malraux, *The Voices of Silence* (1953). Trans. Stuart Gilbert, 13–127. Princeton, N.J.: Princeton University Press.

Marx, Karl. 1963. *The Eighteenth Brumaire of Louis Bonaparte* (1852/1869/1885). New York: International Publishers.

Mulvey, Laura. 1975. "Visual Pleasure and Narrative Cinema." *Screen* 16, no. 3 (October): 6–18.

Noble, Safiya Umoja. 2018. *Algorithms of Oppression: How Search Engines Reinforce Racism.* New York: NYU Press.

Olofsson, Jennie. 2015. "'Did You Mean "Why Are *Women* Cranky?"': Google—A Means of Inscription, a Means of De-Inscription?" In *Between Humanities and the Digital,* eds. Patrik Svensson and David Theo Goldberg, 243–51. Cambridge, Mass: MIT Press.

Parikka, Jussi. 2012. *What Is Media Archaeology?* Cambridge, U.K.: Polity.

Parks, Lisa, and Nicole Starosielski, eds. 2015. *Signal Traffic: Critical Studies of Media Infrastructures.* Urbana: University of Illinois Press.

Posner, Miriam. 2016. "What's Next: The Radical, Unrealized Potential of Digital

Humanities" (2015). In *Debates in the Digital Humanities 2016,* eds. Matthew K. Gold
and Lauren F. Klein, 32–41. Minneapolis: University of Minnesota Press.

Reynolds, Simon. 2011a. "Excess All Areas." *The Wire* 328 (June): 30–5.

Reynolds, Simon. 2011b. *Retromania: Pop Culture's Addiction to Its Own Past.* New York: Faber and Faber.

Rosen, Philip, ed. 1986. *Narrative, Apparatus, Ideology: A Film Theory Reader.* New York: Columbia University Press.

Sekula, Allan. 1986. "The Body and the Archive." *October* 39 (Winter): 3–64.

Starosielski, Nicole. 2015. *The Undersea Network.* Durham, N.C.: Duke University Press.

Terranova, Tiziana. 2004. *Network Culture: Politics for the Information Age.* London: Pluto Press.

Weaver, Warren. 1998. "Recent Contributions to the Mathematical Theory of Communication" (1949). In Claude E. Shannon and Warren Weaver, *The Mathematical Theory of Communication* (1948/1949), 1–28. Urbana: University of Illinois Press.

Archives of Inconvenience

Rick Prelinger

Once upon a time—but whether in the time past or time to come is a matter of little or no moment—this wide world had become so overburdened with an accumulation of worn-out trumpery, that the inhabitants determined to rid themselves of it by a general bonfire. The site fixed upon at the representation of the insurance companies, and as being as central a spot as any other on the globe, was one of the broadest prairies of the West, where no human habitation would be endangered by the flames, and where a vast assemblage of spectators might commodiously admire the show. . . .

"See!—see!—what heaps of books and pamphlets!" cried a fellow, who did not seem to be a lover of literature. "Now we shall have a glorious blaze!"

"That's just the thing," said a modern philosopher. "Now we shall get rid of the weight of dead men's thought, which has hitherto pressed so heavily on the living intellect that it has been incompetent to any effectual self-exertion. Well done, my lads! Into the fire with them! Now you are enlightening the world, indeed!" . . .

The truth was, that the human race had now reached a stage of progress so far beyond what the wisest and wittiest men of former ages had ever dreamed of, that it would have been a manifest absurdity to allow the earth to be any longer encumbered with their poor achievements in the literary line. Accordingly a thorough and searching investigation had swept the booksellers' shops, hawkers' stands, public and private libraries, and even the little book-shelf by the country fireside, and had brought the world's entire mass of printed paper, bound or in sheets, to swell the already mountain bulk of our illustrious bonfire. . . .

—Nathaniel Hawthorne, "Earth's Holocaust"

Fever and Fervor

On those eternally nagging questions of #archives theory, I suggest
we stop "posing questions" and instead propose tentative answers.
—@footage, 2015-10-28[1]

Archive fever is not the same as archival fervor. Archives today are
the center of much attention but few agendas. Archivists, users
and theorists of archives, artists and scholars say much about the
record and its keeping, but their voices rarely reach the public or
leak across disciplinary boundaries. Even if these conversations
were to coalesce, it is unlikely that the speakers would share a
common conceptual or discursive toolbox. And if it were not for
those working archivists who demand respect as both thinkers and
practitioners, the intensity of contemporary interest in archives
would be unmatched by any commitment to intervene in archival
futures. We have reached a swirling stasis, where archives are
active objects of contemplation and contestation, but largely left
to themselves to craft their future shape and negotiate with those
whose futures will be shaped by their recordkeeping efforts.

To argue that archives can inform the redistribution of power
and resources, to advocate that archival theory and practice must
converge, to insist on the recognition of archives as material places
of gendered, racialized labor and poorly examined workflows, and
to engage in actionable as well as notional archival critique—these
are all assertions that we owe to thoughtful archivists more than
to artists and scholars. We ask more from theories of knowledge
than from the institutions where knowledge resides, and while
we fetishize books and libraries, we all too often take for granted
archives and the raw records they hold. Yet for reasons we should
already know and others we have yet to learn, archives need our
active support and continuing engagement. We therefore need to
dive below a surface of platitudes and case-study narratives that
elevate anecdote over argument, and plot a course, no matter
how jagged, for memory institutions in an age of precarities and
rising waters, whether it be to negotiate uncertain alliances or

pursue fragile autonomies. And, even as it may sometimes feel paradoxical, we need to find ways to break through the strictures that bind archives and enclose their contents while simultaneously celebrating the affordances of inconvenience.

Occasions for Excitement

> Archival work & creative practice have converged, which isn't to say artists resemble archivists. Rather, archivists are the new artists.
> —@footage, 2012–10–07

> But does the feverish world of archival innovation resemble Paris in the 1920s, or the USSR in the 1920s?
> —@footage, 2012–10–07

The recent history of archives is replete with inspiring stories of emergence and visibility, but it's also a tale of neglect, of utopian cards unplayed, of disrespect for archival labor, and of theories often too diffuse to be actionable. The gap between actual and potential may help explain why anxiety has become the default mindset in the archival world. Despite these conditions, I'm optimistic about the possibilities that archives afford, not only as bridges between remembrance and action but as arenas of encounter and mobilization. Of all archival affordances we might imagine, historical intervention is perhaps the most exciting: in simplest terms, deploying records of the past in the present so as to influence possible futures. And while power accommodates resistance in symbolic spaces because it is easier to assimilate than resistance in the streets, the record itself is well suited to enable the most pointed and potent of rebukes. And as I will discuss later, evidence offers venues for uneffaced differences to play, opportunities for contestation and critique, and the wherewithal for rendering the excesses of narrativization obsolete.

My intervention—which I explicitly characterize as meditation modulated by provocation—seeks to position archives as places of possibility, as places where we might seek to perform struggle, expose presentism, make theories actionable, refuse dominant narratives of inevitability, and imagine and stage a broad spectrum of futures.[2] In a time when prolepsis and analepsis cycle rapidly, when boundaries between past/present/future manifest as blurred and even invisible, repositories of records are at once anchorages and launchpads and spaces for retrospect and rehearsal. They are the waysides where media temporarily reposes before it is reborn. And today archives are more than reflectors of extrinsic activity: they have also become laboratories where key social and cultural discourses are proposed, argued, and tested. I therefore hope that through more conscious and less isolated archival practices we may better combat the divide between theory and practice and the power relations this divide reinforces. I complete this text in the hot and fiery summer of 2018, unable to know whether archives will survive their current caretakers or whether our successors (or even ourselves) will watch the record-trail of our species fade away. The futures we theorize cannot be based simply on flows of money and power but must also take into account both species fragility and environmental precarity. If archives are to ride the rising waves, it won't be as arks fully caulked to repel leaks but as permeable wetlands capable of assimilating ebbs and flows— venues where past, present, and future interchange and transform one another. In this lies their greatest purpose and occasion for excitement.[3]

> Archival work is generally taken for granted as a kind of infrastructural activity, but we no longer take water & energy for granted #saa12
> —@footage, 2012–08–11

Overtheorized and Underfunded

> The "archive" is overtheorized; "archives" (where the labor of record keeping takes place) are undertheorized and underfunded. #archives
> —@footage, 2015–02–03

Archivists are confounded by the imprecision that exists between "archives," which most archivists define as places of collecting, preservation, access, and archival labor, and "the archive," which I will propose as an umbrella term for conceptual, philosophical, artistic, literary, historical, or analytical constructs centered around archives and/or archival process. I don't consider the two terms interchangeable. Most writers and artists have gravitated to the term "archive." Some also use "the archive" and "the archives" interchangeably without interrogating possible differences. But the fuzziness surrounding "the archives" and "the archive" vexes archivists, who rightfully cringe when the specificity of their workplaces— which are places of labor, not conceptual formulations—is simultaneously invoked and ignored. An unstable amalgam of the unconscious and quotidian, "the archive" has become an undemanding construct, deployed by the critical disciplines as they interact with history and memory, invoked time and again without necessarily requiring sharp definition, similar perhaps to a screen onto which traces of theory flash for long moments before fading.

"The archive" invites flirtation; the "archives," on the other hand, could not be more demanding. Though their workplaces may seem quiet and their workflows pretend to appear apolitical, archives overflow with contention. To collect is to commit to the survival of certain records over others; to arrange and describe is often to enclose; to preserve is to resist power, violence, and constraint; to proffer access can be to invite misunderstanding and aggression. And yet archives yearn for praxis; even routine archival labor is practice in search of theory. But to how many outsiders is all of this visible and, moreover, urgent?

"The archive" seeks to distance itself from "the archives," fleeing the inconvenience of material objects and highly gendered and racialized archival labor. For artists, writers, and theorists, "the archive" is like the Detroit that new occupiers and tourists believe they see: a fascinating, exotic wilderness where historical narratives manifest in disconnected, free-to-remix fragments, populated by people whose needs and agency are matters left for others to address; a place visitors believe to be *terra nullius,* open for unchallenged occupation. Just about any contemporary artist-built collection of images, objects, data, or emotions is nonspecifically designated "an archive," as if to add glamor to assembly. And while artists and scholars express deep fascination with archives and thrill at touring them, they don't think very imaginatively about real ones.[4] With few exceptions, scholars see archives as cabinets of curiosities or as glorified warehouses, service organizations tasked with enabling their research, and they outsource the maintenance of their research base to workers whom they insufficiently respect.

My polarized treatment of these terms is not meant to express contempt but rather hope for their reunification and the reconnection of the practices to which they refer. Could we try to reconcile the conceptual umbrella we call "the archive" with the more quotidian work of "the archives"? Could we daylight both archival theory and practice, construct and workplace? And could we try to draw connections between academic, artistic, and archival labor? This would require greater engagement with archives as working entities, and a commitment not only to rendering archival labor visible, but seeing it as decisive.[5] We might listen harder to the people who perform archival labor and begin to reframe it as cultural work and research in its own right, rather than simply wage labor. Archives are indeed microcosms of the world whose records they contain and organs through which power is expressed, but power and the labor maintaining it exist in covalent bondage. Just as we cannot think of domesticity without domestic labor, and we cannot imagine the university without workers supporting other workers who are paid to produce knowledge, we can neither conceive of nor critique archives without taking into account the core labor of those who maintain them.[6]

Too few have considered the politics of archival workflow. This alone would establish cause for intervention, but the problem may be more fundamental than that. A nuanced and actionable understanding of how day-to-day archival workflow both mirrors and sustains external structures of power requires the kind of attention that art historians might pay to brushstrokes, film theorists to editing rhythms, and psychologists to microaggressions. How do the protocols of archival film inspection, the removal of staples from archival documents, and best practices of photographic scanning contribute to power differentials and influence the way in which archival records can be perceived, touched, and reused?[7] Because there are no clean records: records bear the markers not only of their creators and those who may have used them as levers of power but also bear the traces of their archival lives. We should not expect our future archival queries to return us unmediated records. We might instead hope to see traces of workflow and markers of the record's life in the same way we see scratches on old film, scribbling in old textbooks, tearstains on old letters, and the injuries levied by war and conflict.

Utopian Propositions

> At stake . . . are not the worlds these collections claim to represent, but . . . the worlds they invite us to imagine & even realize #ArchiveFail
> —@bspalmieri, 2014–11–10[8]

Could we discard our predispositions and instead propose a few whimsical and utopian archival propositions?

—A storage and delivery infrastructure for evidence and memory that is as reliable as city water or gravity-propelled Roman sewage systems and flexible enough to remember or forget as needed

—A data corpus that surrounds us like air, manifesting itself through our sensorium and the tools with which we augment our bodies; alternatively, a mycelial network that feeds on data to propagate and spread

—Loci of preservation of information and ideas capable of collecting both the canonical and the quotidian, personal and institutional, hegemonic and oppositional

—An anticipatory network that sniffs out, appraises, and collects records of potential interest

—A fully permeable repository that supports a spectrum of access from casual inquiry to deep touching

—An agnostic system that dissolves formalistic distinctions between physical and digital materials

—A suite of preservation functions that simultaneously support centralized and decentralized storage schemes

—A repository that embodies the power of the record while simultaneously disavowing it, that is to say invoking both privilege and antiprivilege

—A curatorial algorithm that doesn't automatically reject garble and glitch

—A utility that familiarizes us with its holdings through convenience and defamiliarizes them through inconvenience

—An entity that in its scope and outreach crosses anachronistic species boundaries

Even those who never dream of utopia recognize that traditional archives deliver much less than they might. They're compromised by their institutional parentage and bureaucratic structure, gated rather than hospitable, excessively deferential to copyright claims that may never materialize from rightsholders that may not exist, and underresourced islands of precarity in a rich world. These deficiencies separate archives from scholars, who can't always get the records they want in the timeframe and manner they want; from the young, who don't accept pre-Internet limits on information access; and from communities whose records are separated from them forever, enclosed by irrevocable deeds of gift, physical barriers, and access regulations.[9]

But short of utopias, there could be other models. Archives as cities. Could we better understand the trajectories, flows, inputs, outputs, and power relations embedded in and reproduced by archives by thinking of them in the ways we think of cities? To amplify: archives grow, flourish, die, and morph much like cities do. Both, of course, are repositories of information, experience, and dynamic affect. Both are meccas where unaffiliated records and people find community with others; both are machines of encounters, exchanges, mashings-up. Both take in information and energy and transform it. Both combine territories of enclosure with tracts of openness, abiding under a spectrum of control that is constantly pulsing and sliding as authority reconfigures itself. And in both deference to power coexists with hospitality to resistance. Might we look to the city as a way to better understand the relationship of the record to the present? And might we look to archives as a laboratory for constructing new urbanist schemes? Archives, after all, are a cheaper arena than architecture.[10]

On the other hand, are utopian propositions just another projection of external intentions onto the archives, treating them as *terra nullius*? As a professional archivist told me in 2012, "I just like to arrange things."

Do Physical Objects Have a Right to Exist?

Reporting from northern New Jersey: it's a frightfully cold winter morning in January 2011, and I'm driving through an industrial area on a road that disappears and reappears, trying to steer between giant ice ponds and the deepest potholes I've ever seen. The Manhattan skyline isn't very far away—perhaps six miles or so—but if that's the center of the media industry, this is the edge, the place where inconvenient objects go to die. Hidden somewhere in this snowy backwater are the vaults where major movie studios, networks, and distributors store what remains of their nitrate film collections. Municipal fire codes zoned nitrate film out of most major cities many years ago, except for a handful of grandfathered facilities that were built in the early twentieth century. My destination is one of the two commercial nitrate storage facilities left on the East Coast, which has been sold and is soon to become just another obsolete North Jersey industrial site. Right now specially trained truckers are waiting with engines running to move film someone still wants to own somewhere else. I'm here for the same reason I've haunted film vaults and loading docks in the Rust Belt and the Northeast for almost thirty years: to pick up a collection nobody wants. It's hard to believe people aren't clamoring to save this material, but they're not. No matter how wonderful might be the images it holds, this is nitrate film, and it's a thoroughly undesirable commodity.

While few people know much about the fine points of archival practice, just about everybody's heard about the flammability of nitrate film, and this has given rise to the widespread misconception that old film is inherently dangerous. Like most urban legends, those that have spawned around nitrate can be traced back to actual events and partial truths. Huge fires have erupted in film exchanges (warehouses holding films to be sent out to theaters) and projection booths. And yes, several tons of nitrate X-ray film stored in the Cleveland Clinic basement and ignited by an uncovered 100-watt light bulb caught fire in May 1929, killing 123 people, mostly by asphyxiation from the gas that burning nitrate emits.[11] And it's indeed true that water won't extinguish nitrate fires: filmed experiments, legendary among archivists, show burning reels submerged in water, bubbling under the surface as the film generates its own oxygen, and raised from the water only to rekindle into bright flame. Nitrate is indeed hazardous material, and it needs special attention when stored, transported, projected, and copied. But much of the fuss over nitrate film is starting to look more like a moral panic than a safety issue.[12] And what I'm going to learn on this visit to the vaults is that the nitrate film issue perfectly exemplifies a question that I think is about to move from bubbling to burning: do physical objects have a right to exist?

Archivists are drawn to nitrate as to an unstable partner; beautiful and dangerous, nitrate embodies all the clichés of bipolarity. Experienced archivists inculcate emerging archivists with a sense of caution as they stand at their benches winding rolls of film. But while pragmatic hazmat precautions are one thing, nitrate's long-term influence on archivists' senses of self and mission is quite another. A dramatist seeking to find archetypal characters in the archives might first unpack the mystique of nitrate, whose flammability masks far more subversive powers.[13]

Let's stipulate: all media is ephemeral. Nitrate deteriorates and burns with an adrenalin-activating hissy flame; safety-base (acetate) film quietly shrinks and shrivels in irreversible vinegar syndrome; much color film fades; videotape and DVDs flake and rot, and as yet we have no proven strategies for preserving the uncountable number of bits that we're accumulating in the digital era. But nitrate's ephemerality is sensational, mythological. Pioneer film archivists often hid films from fire marshals who might want to destroy them and copyright holders that might want to seize them, and this mixture of caution and stealth imbued archival culture with a deep sense of archivist-as-guardian and archivist-as-last-chance-savior. Relevant keywords: secrecy, fragility, jeopardy, urgency. When U.S. archivists started to decloset and coordinate film preservation efforts under the banner of the American Film Institute in the 1970s, they sought a soundbite for public consumption, and reformulated Canadian archivist Sam Kula's battle cry "Nitrate Will Not Wait" into "Nitrate Won't Wait!" Likening film to a critically endangered whooping crane that might, if neglected, turn into an extinct ivory-billed woodpecker, archivists portrayed themselves as the last line of defense against time and decomposition, heroically snatching film foot by foot from its seemingly inevitable destiny. Since hardly anyone else had stepped forward to systematically preserve films at that point, this wasn't an inaccurate characterization, but the exact nature of nitrate's impatience remained mysterious. To this day we know far too little about the chemistry of nitrate deterioration, though we have at least discovered that cold and dry storage dramatically lengthens the life of film. Widely disseminated statistics (still repeated today, though now understood to be exaggerated) proclaimed that 90 percent of silent film heritage had disappeared.[14] Film studies and film fandom internalized a permanent discourse of loss as cinephiles lamented the disappearance of works they would never see. And in the same way that exaggerated reports of child molestation gave rise to "no touching" rules in schools, film retreated into archives, becoming a hothouse flower to be handled as little as possible, untouchable except by anointed archivists. Perhaps the preservation movement needed a moral panic to take root, but the legacy of the nitrate scare, combined with bureaucratic inertia and fears of copyright infringement, has been to institutionalize archival enclosure. Because film needs to be preserved to be protected, most archival holdings cannot be seen or used unless they've first undergone one or another expensive process: digitization or film-to-film preservation. This is also true for deteriorating videotapes that can't survive repeated plays, as they're being digitized or preserved into another format.

I've come to the Kearny vaults to pack and move two stock-footage libraries that once belonged to Hollywood studios. We've all seen this kind of material time and again without thinking to ask what it is. While the kinds of film I collect and sell for stock footage use revel in their antiquity, studio stock footage is stealthy; it's not supposed to call attention to itself. The intention is for us to believe the studio actually sent a camera crew to Shanghai, to the Lower East Side, or to the North Pole expressly for the film we're watching. Material shot for one picture, if sufficiently generic and free of known performers' faces, was salvaged and meticulously indexed for possible use in future films. Stock footage archives are among the least celebrated image collections, but their contents delight: there are locations around the world, including incredible documentation of U.S. cities in the 1930s and 1940s, cans full of galloping horses' hoofs, gangsters' cars swerving around corners, hands firing revolvers, mirror balls rotating, and miniature models of buildings swaying in simulated earthquakes. And—most exciting of all—there are the process plates.[15]

When classic-era actors rode in a taxi, sat in a dining car, flew a plane, or fled the sheriff's posse, a rear projection of the world

moved behind them. Specially shot scenes—process plates—were
projected on background screens in front of which they performed.
Since actors and screens weren't in the same focal plane, the backgrounds often seemed out of focus, jumpy, distorted in the films
as released. But when you view the process plates by themselves,
they couldn't be clearer—they're rocksteady, razor sharp, detail-
rich images of a world that no longer exists. As I write, I'm watching
one: it's 5th Street in downtown Los Angeles, sometime in the early
1940s. Fifth Street was Skid Row then, and today it's still a sad, dis-
enfranchised slice of the city, most of its small stores and houses
demolished in favor of blank-walled structures hiding social-service
organizations or light-industrial shops. But in the world revealed
by the process plate, we ride around the block with camera set at
a three-quarter reverse angle, enjoying a relaxed, meditative view
of a sidewalk where working-class men amble and storekeepers
take the air outside their shops. This isn't a fleeting image of a lost
landscape that we wish could have lasted longer, but a sixty-second
immersion in the past that enables universal time travel. Along
the way the camera car passes a hand-painted wall advertisement
promoting a natural-foods restaurant. "Live a Hundred Years," the
ad promises.

There are thousands of process plates in this collection. They're
perfectly suited to establish locations in historical documenta-
ries, and perhaps more interestingly, serve as backgrounds and
templates for new digital simulations of the past. But they can
also play all by themselves. I want to use them to strengthen the
case for using unedited footage as an element in itself—to help
establish a new evidentiary cinema that's based on information,
not simply on actors and stories, and to help rethink the structure
of documentary films. Following the lead of retired Berkeley
scholar Bertrand Augst, I have always thought of films not simply
as seamless, extended narratives but rather as instances of
parataxis—assemblies of semi-autonomous segments that one
might liken to walls built from irregularly shaped bricks. Now, many
miles away from a classroom, I will see vaults filled with cans filled

with leftover segments stored away after completion of the films for which they were shot. I will see alternate takes of films by many famous directors; dogfight footage from wartime films whose titles many of us remember; atmospheric scenes of San Francisco shot for noirish features, and can after can of outtakes from Westerns: horses in the pen, desert scenes, pans over mountainous land-scapes. There is three-strip Technicolor, two-strip Cinecolor, and single-strand 35mm monopack, a delicately beautiful film stock much like Kodachrome that was never directly projected onto a screen and flourished so briefly that even the deepest film buffs have rarely seen it.

I arrive at this low-slung complex of twenty vaults marked only with a hand-painted street address, located behind a gate that no longer closes and in front of a creek that occasionally overflows onto the cans stored on the bottom racks. For a moment I'm at a loss trying to find the office, until I realize it's the only door that's not an old steel-jacketed asbestos fire door secured with a padlock. Inside this small, worn room sit Bill and Mike, the two vault managers, whose kindness and sense of humor seem completely unaffected by the certain knowledge that their redundancy is imminent. Today they're working with a group of experienced truckers, members of a tiny group of elite movers who handle nitrate shipments between vaults and archives. No ordinary cargo, nitrate is treated as hazardous material. While it travels via ordinary freight carriers, federal regulations require hazmat-trained personnel to prepare and pack it, according to protocols that seem more suited to nuclear materials than outdated entertainment. Nobody recounts urban legends about nitrate and its flammability this morning, but the vault managers are having a great time pulling up YouTubes of truck accidents, especially wrecked hazmat transports.

Outside the vaults, a group of temporary workers dodge one another on the snowy, narrow catwalk as they pack cans of nitrate film according to federal regulations. After rolling a newly painted steel barrel into position, a worker fills the bottom third of the barrel with urethane packing peanuts. Onto this cushion he lowers a plastic bag containing precisely 18 cans (totaling roughly 18,000 feet, 200 minutes of film) and surrounds the bag with more peanuts. He works a lid into place, tapping it with a mallet to ensure a tight seal, and bolts it tight with a six-inch bolt and a power wrench. As he rolls each barrel up a steep ramp into the waiting trailer, his feet slip and slide on the icy surface. There are 18 cans per barrel, 120 barrels per trailer, 2160 cans per shipment. If it could carry unlimited weight, and if there were no hazmat regulations, the same trailer could carry ten times as many cans. Plastic peanuts blow in the wind, roll under barrels, get ground into pieces by handtruck wheels, and mix into snow and mud. I imagine they'll inhabit the northern New Jersey environment long after all the nitrate has disappeared from the world's cultural repositories.

When the trailer has been loaded to spec, it's the drivers' turn. The companies they work for charge mightily to move nitrate; quotes I've seen come in at about ten dollars per can for a cross-country move. Compared to the costs of destroying unwanted nitrate film, that's small potatoes—legal destruction can cost up to fifty dollars a can, and sometimes destruction is a necessity, especially when the perceived value of the film fails to measure up to the very real difficulties involved in its care. I've never met these drivers before, but as we start to talk I realize they are unsung players in the ecosystems of media management and film preservation. They know the organization and layout of vaults all over the country, which collections they hold, and their custodians. Two of them tell me about the two weeks they just spent in Chicago backing fifty-three-foot trailers through narrow alleys so as to move my friend J. Fred MacDonald's collection when it was acquired by the Library of Congress. While they may not themselves hold archival jobs, they protect and transport some of America's most valuable cultural resources, and act as de facto archivists while film is moving between vaults, the time that it is most vulnerable.

Mike opens the vaults I'm going to be working in. There are five of them, each an unembellished concrete bunker rented by a particular studio or distributor, filled with metal racks on which sit cans of film, some square, some round, some rusty. The rooms are very dirty, and the lights don't always work. At the back of the vault a vent allows air to pass in and out, but its purpose isn't air circulation—it's a relief vent that, in case of a fire, would route an explosive pressure wave out the back of the vault so that the roof won't blow off. The vaults open up directly to the outside world. At one time there was some sort of temperature and humidity control, but it's no longer working, and the owners have decided to rely on the winter weather for the cheapest cooling and dehumidification they can buy.

But first I have to get these cans out of this rather unpleasant and freezing-cold vault. Wedged between two iron pipes, they sit upright, rather than flat on a shelf, as we shelve cans today. This means that the rolls of film inside the cans rest vertically, which may cause them to warp or bend. And since many stock footage cans are shelved on the bottom rack (a testimony to their lack of importance to the studio that sentenced them to dead storage), they've been baptized more than once by the waters of the neighboring creek, and I can see that the down-facing corner of many square cans has rusted out, and that the rolls of film at the bottom of the cans often show signs of mold and immersion.

All of this is being junked by its owners. Some of it, in fact, was junked once before; this is not the first time it's being saved. It might seem odd that its current owners—masters at repurposing old assets for new markets—don't want this material, but it would be unjust to accuse them of a crime against historical memory. They have in fact agreed to donate it to the nonprofit Internet Archive, with whom I work, in order that we may put it online and make it available to today's media makers. But this is only one of many such collections that have become surplus to corporate needs. And their surplusness returns me to my question, which archivists aren't asking, even softly: Do physical cultural objects have a right to exist? Some, like those in this collection, are uncollectible. It is an authentic archives of inconvenience.

Analog, Revalidated and Devaluated

I worry that we won't be strong enough to prevent digital stewardship from becoming analog neglect.

—@footage, 2013–07–23

It's been my good fortune to be able to engage in potlatching, an ancient privilege newly reborn with the Internet, since I began collaborating with Internet Archive in 1999 to build an online repository of freely downloadable archival moving images documenting social relations, persuasion and propaganda, place, race, gender, domesticity, travel, and industry (Prelinger and Internet Archive 2000). A project without a mission statement risks failure or irrelevance but also implies the possibility of constant reframing, and this one has taken unexpected directions. I have seen the barriers that often separate archival collections from those who would use them melt away, and have had the satisfaction of seeing materials that had long sat quietly on steel shelves pushed out to anyone who might be interested. Since its launch at the end of 2000, our online collection has supported approximately 160 million access events. Materials that were once marginalized as dated ephemera have been able to float outside the time and cultural frames in which they were produced and find their way into an unknowable number of derivative works, remixable with or without concern for their historicity. Concurrently, however, these 7,000 moving image files live on the Web to serve the development of visual history, to illustrate and hopefully problematize complex ideas and claims, and to serve the evidentiary needs of existing and emergent social movements. The evidence they embody retains context but is also free to shed its provenance, and this body of complex documentation now lives not simply within a single archival classification and retrieval system but as Net infrastructure, which is the greatest honor an archives can receive. Ultimately I hope the collection will deeply embed itself within digital humanities projects and also serve as a testbed for computationally based projects carried out by posthuman agents. The volume of home movies, for instance, is so great that their second audience (following the families that made them) is likely to be principally composed of analytic machines.

This experience turned me into a rabid proponent of pushing archival materials out to the world regardless of whether there was an expressed or substantiated need. I learned that an archives' highest calling is to be consumed by its users. I tried to convince my moving image archives colleagues to support mass digitization of their collections, and worked with Internet Archive in the mid-2000s to help build out an open path for mass book scanning that functioned as an alternative to Google's then highly closed and secretive books project. Joining a small group of digitization evangelists who fanned out across the Euro-American cultural sphere, I tried to encourage cultural custodians to make peace with digitality and choose openness.

But concurrently I was working with my partner Megan to build a physical library in San Francisco, which has been open to the public since 2004 (Prelinger and Prelinger 2018). To those who have not visited, this may seem strangely retrograde, but it was and is a thoroughly antinostalgic project. Our principal (if unvoiced) idea was to experiment with opening a repository of physical materials to a noninstitutional community and see what might happen. In the absence of a hypothesis the lessons were even more surprising. We learned very quickly to dismiss all sense of analog nostalgia or digital supersession. It became clear that, to transcode a formulation from poet and artist Jen Bervin, physical and digital materials each had different but closely related jobs to do.[16] Analog and digital affordances were not only distinct, but codependent—as it happened, the physical books served as pointers to the downloadable digital copies scanned at Internet Archive, and Google's index of Internet Archive's online books helped us find books on our uncatalogued shelves. It was pointless to overthink the digital turn or to harp on analog/digital antinomies, unless you were talking about obvious attributes like weight, physical bulk, and dependence on electron flow, or unless you needed conflict for an otherwise pedestrian news story. Since then I've been convinced that analog-digital hybridity is not a transitional state, and I'd hope it remains a permanent one. Scanning, after all, is just the newest of the book arts.

In my work with our library and my film archives I've come to realize that the turn to digital revalidates the analog. I make digital films that play before audiences who talk while the film runs. I thought this was radical, until I realized I was actually channeling the Elizabethan theater whose front pit was filled with loud and boisterous groundlings.[17] Hybridized analog and digital. But while digitality may revalidate analog, it's rapidly devaluing it. Physical objects are being disposed of and destroyed at an accelerated rate (which is one reason we've been able to collect so much interesting stuff for our library and so much film has come to us for shipping costs alone). That highly impertinent question for librarians and archivists—do physical objects still have the right to exist?—often seems these days to be settled in the negative. Shelves are emptier and stacks shrunken in many libraries. While collectors responsible to no one but themselves make piecemeal decisions to collect objects that match their fancies, libraries and archives are faced with time-consuming and difficult decisions as to whether to bear the expense of collecting, organizing, cataloging, and preserving dead and dying media. Even if the cost of digitization pursued at scale has dropped, predigitization processing (paging books from the stacks, inspecting materials for fitness before they go through robotically assisted scanning processes, cleaning and preparing reels of film or videotape for scanning, inspecting phonograph records, then performing quality assurance on files and returning source materials to proper shelf locations, and so on) is inherently artisanal and can be costly. Recent experience is also teaching us that scanning is not a one-time process, and that we will rescan originals from time to time as our perceptions of what constitutes an acceptable digital surrogate evolve along with our technical abilities. From the outside, the choices librarians and archivists make may seem easy to criticize, but these are not simple decisions.

Sometimes it's unthinkable to destroy original documents after filming or digitizing them, sometimes not. As with people, society sorts physical objects into classes. At the bottom level are work-aday paper documents designed for specific purposes at specific times: cancelled checks, invoices, technical documentation, letters, and the like. A bit higher ranking (but not that high) are published materials of an ephemeral nature, frequently revised and re-freshed; I'm thinking of telephone directories, newspapers, legal materials, and reference books. Some materials in this category, like *The New York Times,* carry recognized historical importance, but few of them are retained in physical form. Higher still are published materials invested with long-term or permanent value, like schol-arly books, academic journals, many magazines and periodicals, maps, and government documents—though increasingly libraries are planning shared print repositories where a few "copies of last resort" stand in for many widely distributed copies soon to be no more. At the highest level reside rare books, special collections, manuscripts and original photographic images. The emergent sta-tus of digital materials has not yet challenged the auratic primacy of these objects.

And yet—a systematic downgrading of media forms seems to be in progress as the specific affordances of old-fashioned platforms like film, broadcast television, audiotape, and Kodachrome slides are flattening into digital modes of storage and display. I do not mean to minimize the depth, novelty, or importance of digital affordances, but I perceive the disorganized diversity of extinct analog media disappearing into files that (if the walled gardens of the entertainment industry allow) are capable of playing and recombining freely across a plurality of devices. Media that used to rank high on the auratic scale is trickling down; we're witnessing the impoverishment of the genteel classes. Librarians, archivists (and, to be fair, custodians of almost all forms of the historical record) have sinned. They have avoided engagement with records in inconvenient formats; they have deaccessioned, weeded, discarded, recycled, pulped. They have reformatted inconvenient

records into new forms that may for a time seem more compact,
readable, accessible, persistent.

> Today's persistence is tomorrow's ephemerality, just as today's
> ephemerality is tomorrow's persistence. #archives #bewaredigital
> exclusivity
>
> —@footage, 2018–03–31

The crisis ecosystem of evidence-bearing physical objects and
their displacement in favor of digital surrogates is akin to urban
gentrification, and as scholars and as a society we will one day
have to answer for it. The attributes of physical materials like
books and vinyl records are not falling out of use, even if they
have lost their universality. I cannot completely describe the many
affordances of books and paper, but they are sufficient to inhibit
the total conquest of e-books.[18] Preserving how we experience and
apprehend the record is as much an archival objective as preserving what the record contains. And the system in which the record is
created, transmitted, and distributed is itself a fragile assembly of
information in need of archival attention. As media archaeologists
look at platforms of production and distribution, they may find the
leaders, cans, and shipping containers that surround films to be of
greater interest than the films themselves.[19]

But no matter how many we successfully discard, physical objects
are incredibly persistent, and their persistence is inconvenient.
They're the table scraps, the leftovers of digitization, and there
aren't enough dogs around the table to gobble them down. We are
basing entire new phenomenological and philosophical agendas (to
say nothing of how we configure scholarship) on one single itera-
tion of technology—the digital turn—and we seem to be fighting a
scorched-earth path through physical materials in order to make
room for apparent digital abundance.

This issue was very much on my mind several months before I visited the nitrate vault in New Jersey, and as I got more and more en-
thusiastic about the neglected cans nobody wanted, I remembered

a story I had recently heard during THATCamp in San Francisco, a loose "unconference" attended by scholars, geeks, librarians, and archivists, attempting to get people collaborating on digital humanities tools and projects. Archives were a recurrent topic, and there was tremendous interest in leveraging archival holdings to enable new scholarship, build new applications, and modulate the physical world with historical data using augmented-reality technology. There were also provocative moments. My big takeaway turned out to be a throwaway, a comment tossed off during yet another discussion about the importance of metadata—data that describes the contents and structure of information, or perhaps more easily remembered, "data about data." Someone who had previously worked at an unsuccessful mapping data company explained what happened when the company closed down and its workers rushed to find safe homes for its assets, which were mostly data. This, he told us, was difficult, and it was harder because of the need to describe the contents and organization of the data to potential purchasers. "Data," he said, "is a liability."

Tape is a liability. Film is a liability. These are incendiary statements. It might be more precise to say that "aging data is a liability," or that "old media is a liability." But just as a society should judge itself by how well it takes care of its most vulnerable members, archivists might similarly dedicate themselves to collecting, preserving, and providing access to words, images, and sounds fixed in dead or dying media. Archivists are in the same position today as the brave librarians who guarded in vain hundreds of millions of volumes like *Congressional Record,* 1920s-era romance novels, and old telephone books. Whether or not digitization and destruction of inconvenient materials is appropriate is indeed a difficult question, but that's a question for a discussion that rarely seems to happen. In the past, I've suggested that we take a leaf from environmentalism and require "digitization impact statements" and "preservation impact statements" when we undertake grand projects, in order to better understand their broad cultural and historical impact (Prelinger 2010). In any case, I don't think that decisions to migrate and destroy material should be made in private. While a single decision may seem trivial or obvious, the sum of many decisions will change history.

> May I just say it again: Loss is to be avoided when possible, but it's also formative. New histories arise around loss. #pda15 #pda2015
> —@footage, 2015–04–24

> @mchris4duke: Marginalized, persecuted people have had to destroy their own history for their safety. Loss isn't random. #rbms15
> —@john_overholt, 2015–06–26[20]

I do not universally mourn the loss of physical records. While I condemn intentional destruction of records in order to suppress histories and annihilate identities, I've come to believe that loss can be formative. Absences, too, may be necessary to protect marginalized communities and their cultures, as I will note later. We pursue research precisely because we perceive gaps in the record, or because we come to recognize that the powerful have suppressed evidence about the powerless. Many of the emergent histories of the last fifty years (African American, womens', labor, daily life, and disability, to cite just a few) have moved toward the scholarly center precisely because the need was felt to remediate disappearance or absence. We must learn to work with inevitable loss and, as many archivists have suggested, render absences in the archives as prominent as presences, while sometimes recognizing their necessity. The analog losses we mourn today will be as nothing compared to the digital losses we are already beginning to experience.

Destabilized Digitality

> @footage: "the archivist's job is to hack media, so that it can be preserved against its will." #orphans10
> —@snowdenbecker, 2016–04–07[21]

I have so far mostly spoken of physical materials. Don't digital materials permit us to slip the surly bonds of paper and film and touch the face of data itself?

Digitality is inconvenient in its own ways. Despite its apparent victory over physicality, digitality is fragile. It requires a compliant social order, the accommodation of governments, and the steady availability of energy. It is not a monolith; the Chinese digital world works differently than the North American. And its corporate structures and business models are experimental. We cannot overreact today to a force that will behave differently tomorrow.

The air of romantic obsolescence that surrounds a lot of historical media and communications technology today carries quite an allure, and we might actually enlist it to help build a bridge between media archaeologists and the public, but it isn't quite as defamiliarizing as some media archaeologists might suggest. While landscapes of deindustrialized cities are rich texts filled with evidentiary threads implicating many players, most visitors see only ruin porn.[22] Dead media, failed kludges, speculative engineering ventures that pass neither usability nor smell tests and express poorly integrated relationships between information and its embodiments are all deeply fascinating, but we need to squeeze those "neglected margins" hard. And yet anything we can do to alienate the unreasonable faith much of the world seems to have in the robustness and persistence of the digital would be most welcome. As long, perhaps, as we are not fetishizing the digital glitch, the drop-out, the rotten bit. For digital media whose persistence depends on recurrent and heroic human intervention, preservation itself is the ultimate glitch, far more consequential than any scrambled screen.

Many archivists also fetishize extinct media technologies. They are the ones buying all those old film projectors. They sit up at night worrying not about their eBay overspending but about digital precarity. The archival axioms of permanence and provenance don't remap well into the digital domain, where everything is as fragile as the next spike, brownout, or coronal mass ejection and bits thought to be lost can resurface in forgotten directories. In the aggregate, archivists have thought a great deal about the implications and contradictions of digital archives, but like many who present as futurists, they have yet to reflect on how these peculiar datasets will function socially.

Digital archives are already pervasive. They might be total—meaning they are not simply reservoirs of information that supports power but organs of power as well, like transmission lines that store as well as propagate energy (Jardine and Kelty 2016). Both archivists and nonarchivists try to track and parse the disruptions that digital media and repositories have brought to the disciplines that our predecessors (and even some of us, if we're old enough) secretly hoped we could follow in peace and privilege until our temporary abilities faded. And digital archives embody archival inconvenience skinned in new interfaces. It's all too evident that engineers have a great deal to do with the design of digital archives; they tend to route around what they perceive as inconvenience. The early 2010s will be remembered as a time when the ease (if not the precision) of Google searches rendered older databases inadequate, and the first hit more often than not was the greatest hit. Google's deep pockets enabled the company to hide great intelligence behind a deceptively simple search box, which we now expect to see on almost every webpage even if we don't quite understand where and how it probes. At the same time digital libraries are still industriously writing grants to simulate the serendipity produced for free in library stacks.

As digital repositories become more complex and diverse, they get harder to classify. The databases become soupier, less structured. The loci of intelligence shifts from structured data to smarter queries, as I surmise we're seeing with Google searches. But the engineering goal remains the same: to link queries more closely to results. This is hard for the flâneur in me to accept. What happened to the cyberpunk idea of oneness, of *being* the data, of jacking (hacking) into datasets whose bits directly acted on the senses? There's little serendipity in the hidden algorithms tucked away in a black box. In their insatiable hunger for facts as distraction, Bouvard and Pécuchet would have warmed to the Web for its linkability, but I imagine Google would have frustrated them; a machine that always returned answers to specific questions instead of setting them on excursions into wholly new disciplines would have rendered impossible the intellectually picaresque journey of the two copy clerks and denied the novel its reason to exist.

Query-based searches are inevitably reductive. Deeper research relies on confronting inconvenience and capitalizing on its attributes. And if we are to resist the intentional dumbing-down of digital tools and services, we have little recourse but to return, once in awhile, to analog materials.

> I once thought digital would define classical language & analog the vulgar tongue, but I now think the opposite is starting to come true.
> —@footage, 2013–08–15

Reverse digital divide: At times I've felt part of a digital vanguard: making CD-ROMs with the Voyager Company in the early and mid-1990s. Putting archival films online. Scanning books from our little library. Feeling for my friends on the other side of what was then a digital crevasse. But now it's different. Digitality and privilege have been inverted. Speaking personally with a bureaucrat, collecting and touching artisanal objects, writing with a fountain pen—these are privileged encounters. The rest of the world wrestles with voicemail menus, cheaply made goods, and poorly designed governmental websites. There are no stray bits in your slow food. And slow media is all the rage. Some friends are building an intentional community in Mendocino County, on the northern California coast. They're installing fiber on their farm, but it transmits data slowly, and when I visited, their Internet service went on between 6:00 and 7:30 am and midnight to 2:00 am. One of the consequences of the universalization of digital labor and the blurring of the barrier between online work and recreation may well be a retreat from digitality by those who can afford to do so.

Stories and Theories

> If we really believe humans are a "storytelling species" why do entertainers, filmmakers, curators repeat this statement so incessantly?
> —@footage, 2013–08–18

Our newly ex-Librarian of Congress James Billington liked to say:
"Stories unite people, theories divide them" (quoted in Mariano and
Norton, 2011). I always hoped for the opposite to come true. As
Brecht hoped for his epic theater, I place high priority on dividing
the audience, and at least for a time I hoped the world would unite
around certain theories. And I remain unconvinced of the centrality
and absolute value of what today many people call "storytelling."
Storytelling, ubiquitous in almost all documentary and historical
media intended for public consumption, is characterized by a highly traditional representational strategy that may include the om-
nipresence of characters (often good and evil) and a conventional
act-based narrative arc in which seemingly insurmountable problems are generally solved (Prelinger 2009). It is often stated that
storytelling is hardwired in human consciousness, but I disagree; I
believe it is acculturated and culturally specific. The ambiguity and
enigmatic nature of images and evidence, which might take us in
so many directions, is forced into the most opportune channel to
establish a story that can be told within the bounds of budget and
mass comprehension, a story that succeeds and thus contributes
to a sort of narrative triumphalism. Not every tale is treated fairly
by this tactic. And in fact most of the evidence we see drawn from
archives is overtold, encrusted with narrative. By contrast, I seek to
find a place for foregrounding the record itself with relatively little
"storytelling." In other words, I attempt to encourage new kinds of
negotiation between the document and its users, and let a more-
or-less contextualized, or even decontextualized document find its
own path. This could mean trusting evidence over interpretation.
Evidence can be its own narrative; storytelling is a special interest.

I work by arranging evidence as best I can. For the past ten years,
I have made films out of home movies and other archival film
materials without using music, sound design, narration, or visual
effects. I rely on audiences to make their own soundtrack—in other
words, to talk their way through my films. I encourage them to
identify familiar places, people, and events; to ask questions; to
dispute the assertions of their neighbors; to find a place for their

voices in the film while it is playing, and thus to determine where and how the film progresses. Home movies play a key role in these films. Evidence might be trustworthy in the morning and devious in the afternoon, and the editor's grip might vary in strength, but there is something irreducibly honest about a document made by a nonprofessional who is motivated, as with most home movie makers, by love for their subject. This is not a universal stance or a normative form of filmmaking, but avoiding overnarrativization lets me breathe more freely, and it validates archival documents over storylines that may have little to do with the documents themselves.[23]

Archives could push back against the terms that restrain how far publicly practiced and received histories can stretch. To do this doesn't just mean foregrounding underrepresented narratives and records that have been suppressed by force and violence, but actively daylighting records that represent anomalies, that document uneffaced differences—personalities, cultures, and technologies that don't fit into simplistic, dominant timelines and that refute narratives of triumphalism and progress—and allow them to play freely. Home movies, of course, exemplify this kind of record in the way that they simultaneously document and resist interpersonal commonalities, presenting powerful evidence of race, gender, class, and place whose granularity of detail and richness of expression often cannot be comprehended through shallow and stereotypical interpretations. We are only beginning to realize the potential of home movies (and I extend this to personally generated records of all kinds) to challenge not only existing historiographies but existing dramaturgies as well, and I believe home movies offer one key to rendering the excesses of narrativization obsolete.

> I think the covert function of an archive is to make things more complex, to complicate, to serve as a counterbalance to the reductive and endlessly repeated soundbites that constitute much of what we are told is "history."
> (Darms 2015)

No one is likely to halt the trend toward narrativizing evidence.
At its simplest it is like sorting eggs, and this renders it likely that
wholesale narrativization will be done by machines on the fly, in the
same way that Storify builds a thin narrative crust out of a tweet-
stream or low-budget news services draft bots to write stories. And
there will obviously be fancier tools, some of them that may gain
credence as default means to touch or to construct windows into
archival content. Facebook's Timeline is a narrativizing spine whose
genius lay in its merging our personally authored words and images with the record of what we watched, listened to, and bought.
Like the devotees who compiled a complete bibliography of every
book on Bertolt Brecht's shelves (Wizisla, Streidt, and Loeper 2007),
Facebook recognized that our biographies were as much about
what we consumed as what we produced.

> twitter, you're a kaleidoscopic cacophony of fragmentary, illusive
> and momentary information, serving up rumors, fears & wishes
> #Ferguson
>
> —@footage, 2014–08–16

And yet let me rehearse a half-hearted argument in favor of storytelling. It is urgent to preserve and disseminate the histories of
today's civil rights movement. The greatness of these histories lives
in the nature of their creators—grassroots activists, community
members, lay witnesses to historical moments—and in their granularity. These histories are principally built of tiny pieces circulated
through social media: Tweets, Instagrams, Periscope videos of
greater or lesser persistence, calls and responses on Facebook.
The assembly of these fragments forms a history that is as difficult
to make sense of as it is to read a photograph from its halftone
dots. Evidence collides with evidence, generating tangles that
might never be unraveled. Here might be a place for some kind of
storytelling beyond mere chronology. But if we assume that we can
at least display *some* of this material, how do we make it meaningful? How can we respect the evidence without strangling it in
narrative, while making some sense of it without privileging a single

or oversimplified interpretation? This is the single biggest problem we encounter when we select individual archival documents for display—we end up privileging specific narratives, putting answers before questions.

These materials are often sensitive, and their free use may be restricted by terms of service, copyright restrictions, and concerns for the privacy and legal vulnerability of the people who made social media posts or appeared in someone's photos. They may therefore be likely to be restricted to in-house use in a brick-and-mortar archives or museum, just as Library of Congress's Twitter archives, if ever made ready for public display, will be kept offline. In this respect, the new digital archives will tend to resemble the old physical ones. They will propagate only over the Net when people quote what they read or photograph what they see on the walls. But the reason for making archives of these materials is to construct bridges rather than walls. This argues for accessibility, especially if we are to be hospitable to nontraditional archives users. In recent years we have collectively developed a big box of accessibility tools—data visualization and mapping platforms that are accessible to anyone with the computer literacy of the average gamer—and perhaps we can use these tools to narrativize evidence without losing its power along the way. Or, perhaps, to use the occasion of a museum visit to explain how storytelling can be a tool to expand and contract consciousness alike.

> The historical interest of a work is inversely proportional to number of gatekeepers it passes thru. Books vs ephemera; TV vs home movies
> —@footage, 2016–04–27

Personal Records and Vernacular Collecting

> Erika Mijlin: we regard excessive production of data w. celebration & awe, quite unlike way we regard other waste #poeticsandpolitics2015
> —(@footage, 2015–05–17)[24]

Hoarding can express distress & confusion, but also a need for
rootedness & security. This is something for #archives to consider.
#mac16

—@footage, 2016–04–30

Mars's First Hundred settlers in Kim Stanley Robinson's Mars Trilo-
gy discover how to extend the human lifespan by several hundred
years but are unable to get as keen a grip on the bioscience of
memory preservation. Drawn to remediate their amnesia about
events that happened over a century earlier, they frequently search
databases to prompt their fading memories. Interestingly, almost
all the searches target personal rather than institutional records.
From this, and from today's social media–centered Internet, I am
tempted to imagine the characteristics of future database queries.
It seems quite possible that repositories of personal records and
the microhistories associated with individual lives will become far
more pertinent to the needs of future searchers than the records
of government and institutions—especially if surveillance databases are considered as repositories of personal records.

In any case, there's no question that the volume of personal media
production is historically offscale. In such an environment it's really
hard to distinguish the archival from the contemporary. Residual
and emergent, prolepsis and analepsis, not just coexisting but
combining and reframing. Think of YouTube, Facebook, Twitter,
Snapchat, even the sadly languishing Flickr, all pseudo-archives
that have supported quotation and reframing almost from their
beginnings. The majority of personal media production occurs
within these constantly refreshed workspaces that share common
objects with custodial services that pretend to be archives but
whose archival compact with users, as I've said elsewhere, is a
noncommittal handshake (Prelinger 2015). We think we are saving
our videos, photos, and posts, but we're betting in a game where
the house holds an insurmountable advantage. Does the trauma
of archival erasure extend across the full spectrum of loss from
the destruction of a whole society's records to the closedown

of a social media service and the concomitant loss of personal materials? We will unfortunately have the opportunity to ask this again and again.

Personal records have always been intimidatingly infinite relative to the societies that create them. Personal digital materials don't represent a new challenge but rather inhabit a spectrum of personal recordkeeping that begins in the deep analog era: scratches in the sand, drawings on cave walls, clay tablets, papyrus fragments, graffiti, and so on; extending to quilts, diaries, letters, and postcards; then home movies and home video; into contemporary digital media, and finally toward digital and postdigital media we are now seeing and might or might not expect in the future— body cams (Google Glass was only a first effort), location data and metadata from phones, et cetera; CCTV feeds; human metrics, such as the Quantified Selfists collect; endoscopy; sonograms; medical telemetry and, maybe sooner than we think, brain waves. Almost all of these "platforms" gave rise to an abundant record in their time; each posed preservation problems; and long-term survival of the record was rarely an issue.

Personal records are highly granular, typically uncharismatic, eminently unselectable, frequently unreleasable, effectively infinite, extremely inconvenient. Who owns today's personal records? Who maintains them? Who forgets me; how can I be forgotten? There is complex, covert mirroring between records that exist part in open and part in classified worlds, giving rise to the jokes that NSA is our most reliable backup service. The lack of consistency in the way we regard our personal privacy adds to the confusion. It is remarkable how much people are willing to reveal publicly or semipublicly, to "friends." I have speculated that many people are less worried about the original, granular data we spin off as a function of living in networked culture than they are about others transforming it into ordered timelines or narratives. Unsorted, unmodulated evidence may feel less sensitive than coherent stories others build and attach to our identities.[25]

Archivists sometimes express fatalism at personal digital archives conferences. Questions turn into imponderables, and in general archivists (at least those who tweet their thoughts) are loath to invade personal privacy. Consequently they often revert to tool building because the big issues are profoundly complex and the mass of data unknowable to civilians. For a time it may feel safer to make analysis and processing tools and experiment on controllable datasets. But in my most optimistic moments, I think the weight of the quotidian record lifts away when we stop fussing and actually engage with it. The flour, oil, and salt some of us store against the prospect of apocalyptic starvation is easier to refresh when it is regularly drawn from. We will have to somehow make it safe to play with secrets, no matter how difficult the rules of that game may be.

> I'd be curious to hear from anyone who's written or thought about #archival activity as a practice resembling #permaculture
> —@footage, 2012–10–14

Access to personal records is one issue; long-term, infinite-capacity, robust, and sustainable storage another. Recent research proposing DNA as such a solution (Bornholt, Lopez, Carmean, Ceze, Seelig, and Strauss 2016) has piqued the archival imagination; some archivists wanting to believe that data precarity has been fixed, others clinging to risk eternal. I represent the latter category. What might infinite storage mean? The possibility of infinite storage actually invokes all sorts of fascinating problems of abundance. Infinite storage depreciates the value of individual records. Infinite warehouses make it easier to lose individual pallets. Infinite repositories of memory will enable forgetting on an unprecedented scale. Even the prospect of infinite digital storage revalidates the beleaguered physical artifact. Infinite storage will revivify old-school, artisanal-style curation. The paradox of infinite storage is that it will finally convince many of us not to hoard, because when loss is no longer a possibility, surviving records lose their privilege.

Nontransparent societies (most societies, other than perhaps Scandinavian) are unlikely to resolve the question of access to personal records. Archives whose chief raison d'être is to preserve nonstate historical and cultural records seek to be open (however the cultural meaning of "openness" may shift in time and place), and they wish to serve needs that do not explicitly facilitate surveillance and control. But for the moment it is impossible to provide the same kind of access to records with sensitive personal characteristics as to public and institutional records (especially government records that have been released or are statutorily open), and therefore personal records tend to be held under conditions that replicate the traditional inaccessibility of most archival collections. We are seeing this today with records of social movements, such as Occupy and Black Lives Matter. Most would agree that preserving these records is an imperative, but when we look more closely at their content and realize the legal and personal vulnerabilities of identifiable participants in these movements, our reservations grow.

There are other important reasons to keep many records quiet or private. Much traditional knowledge and traditional cultural expression is not intended for sharing outside the community or society in which it was created, and often not meant to be shared between all community members. To expose and disperse knowledge with ceremonial or spiritual significance can be an act of cultural aggression that perpetuates the history of wars against Aboriginal, Indigenous, and Native peoples. Many established repositories hold and expose records whose public visibility offends and endangers traditional communities. "Open access for all, to all" cannot be a culturally universal call.[26]

The paradox, then, is that much of what we must collect must also remain silent. Emerging repositories of personal and community records may inhabit vaults with virtual time clocks corresponding to every person represented in the archives, each ticking toward its own unlocking date. Is this really a situation to avoid?—we might ask. At the very least, it is ironic. The advent of ubiquitous networked digital cultures has forced many cultural and historical

archives to rethink the restrictions they have traditionally placed
on access to their holdings. The Internet's ascendancy has also
drowned us with senses of entitlement and possibility, allowing us
to imagine that, yes, we can in fact collect the traces of all of our
lives. But some of the new collections that can dive deep into our
individual and community's histories and intentions may for now
be too inconvenient to be freely shared.

> I could not forget, in an age of space-ships, world wars &
> publicity, that the real things of the country were hidden
> & inward. (Brooks 1961)

Amateurism

I'm interested in why we don't refer to "personal analog/physical
archiving" but say "collecting" in most cases. #pda12
—@footage, 2012–02–24

Vernacular archival practices by ordinary people are more persistent
than standards and workflows of professional archivists. #archives
—@footage, 2012–02–25

Media archaeologists and anxious industry executives share at
least one attribute, and that's a special concern for media technologies and practices that originate at the periphery of established
media industries. Both keenly track the challenges these may pose
to dominant platforms. In so doing they peek into a future when
suits and brand names may no longer receive the respect to which
they've been accustomed. Archives are equally challenged by
vernacular efforts to collect, manage, and preserve the historical
record, and only the most courageous archivists have looked into
the future and recognized uncoordinated decentralization as
positive. Distributed collecting does raise complicated questions:
it seems likely to me that the archival future will be much more
about the coordination of a mass of collecting efforts than about
the niceties of selection and appraisal; what future digital archivists
are able to save will result from billions of lucky accidents, and one

of their jobs will be to share knowledge of what data persists and keep track of evolving idiosyncratic recordkeeping models.

Popular archival practice doesn't get as much attention as the latest viral video, but it's excitingly disruptive. Personal, independent, and community collections enable research and access in ways that more traditionally organized institutions cannot. They may not be nearly as organized or comprehensive, but they are often more direct and efficient. They may not present our materials on lovingly contextualized and vetted websites but can often shovel a lot of material online to surprise and enrich their users. Nontraditional entities can often be better at collecting specialized materials (nontextual, for instance) that can be vexing to traditional collections. And by defamiliarizing the compartmentation and seemingly mysterious workflows that exist in most special collections, independent collections encourage users and archivists to imagine about how future libraries and archives might work. Of all entities we might call "archival," independent, community and amateur collections come closest to actionable spaces, possessing all the virtues, and of course the flaws, of amateurism.

> For a younger generation of feminists, the archive is not necessarily either a destination or an impenetrable barrier to be breached, but rather a site and a practice integral to knowledge making, cultural production, and activism. The archive is where academic and activist work frequently converge. . . . Rather than a destination for knowledges already produced or a place to recover histories and ideas placed under erasure, the making of archives is frequently where knowledge production begins. (Eichhorn 2013, 3)[27]

Perhaps the firehose of personal records requires centralized institutions that can collect at scale. But already individuals and nonprofessionalized groups are often the first responders and sometimes the most assiduous preservers of personal (and certain impersonal, depending upon their focus) digital materials. If true, we are heading into a delightfully kaleidoscopic period of archival practices, a panorama of outsider collections whose allure will radiate from the methods by which they were collected and organized, rather than by what they may contain. But while this prospect may be enabled by the digital turn, we do not owe its conception to digitality.

The historian Robert C. Binkley promoted amateur scholarship and collecting before his untimely death in 1940 (see Binkley 2016). He characterized amateur historians, collectors, and independent scholars as a kind of citizen research force whose self-motivated efforts (or organized efforts through such agencies as the U.S. Works Progress Administration) could fill gaps in scholarship and collecting unaddressed by established libraries, archives, and universities. Long before E. P. Thompson popularized the phrase "history from below," Binkley addressed the work the academy was leaving undone. In several inspiring essays, replete with suggestions and scenarios we still might consider implementing, he imagined a kind of distributed research and publishing system that opened participation in scholarship to amateurs, the uncre-dentialed, and the unemployed, a system that made use of new reproduction techniques like micropublishing, offset printing, and strike-on typesetting. He promoted (and may have conceived) the WPA program for unemployed intellectuals in Ohio, a public works innovation employing them to inventory local history collections and index historical newspapers. A close reading of his *Manual on Methods of Reproducing Research Materials* (1936), packed with fascinating descriptions of now-extinct technologies that will de-light today's media archaeologists, reveals little foreknowledge of electronics but much anticipation of the attributes of the Internet as a system for scholarly communication, and the turn toward digital humanities.[28]

Archives of Inconvenience

Those talks on archival materials that conclude sanctimoniously, but worst of all *boringly,* that "archives matter":

—@ncecire, 2015–02–28[29]

If all you can get out of your archival materials is that they matter,
then they do not in fact matter.

—@ncecire, 2015–02–28

Archival enclosure is a systemic problem and nonproductive
inconvenience. But other inconveniences can be formative.
Wrangling with inconvenience is like choosing to write by hand
instead of typing or dictating; you learn more about the words you
are processing (see Mueller and Oppenheimer 2014). My urban
history film events have been made possible in part through the
productive inconveniences of physical media. Archival film is often
inconvenient to work with and difficult to see; it takes time, labor,
and resources to inspect, repair, document, prep for scanning,
scan, edit, and so forth. Workflow can, however, be exploited to
bring other interested parties into the production process: it can
involve community members, creators and their relatives, and
possibly even motivated scholars. In the same way a gem cutter
spends time closely examining the uncut stone, engagement with
the physical constituents of a film brings the maker(s) into a closer
relationship with the possibilities the film might express.

Inconvenience enables defamiliarization, which is what makes
movies (and, in fact, all representation) possible. Inconvenience
defamiliarizes not only the deceptive ease of interfacing but
foregrounds the problematics of our relationships to interfaces as
well as the information that lies behind them. Just as engagement
with digital media helps us better understand analog affordances,
engagement with digital inconvenience will allow us in time to
negotiate clearer terms with the digital turn. Rather than trying to
efface the inconvenient attributes of archives, it is time to celebrate
and make our peace with them.

But while welcoming archival inconvenience, we cannot overlook
archival precarity. Most cultural repositories lack strong advocates,
and we must step in to help defend their independence and ensure
their persistence. We must find a way to thematize archives simultaneously in two realms: as players in unpredictably evolving media

ecosystems, and as entities that stand apart from the voracious present and offer at least a fair shot at historical accountability. One plausible strategy for scholars and artists might be to engage rather than outsource: to emulate the labor of entomologists, folklorists, and field recorders, many of whom collect their own research material rather than relying on others to supply it. Placing archival practice at the core of our own work permits us to join with archivists in determining the evolution of recordkeeping. The decentralization (and reengineering) of archival practice should not just be the mission of archives but of their users and supporters as well. The active critique of archival practice cannot prevent us from engaging with archives in all of their imperfection and working to bridge the gaps that have separated repositories from users, theorists, and the public.

What archives offer the contemporary mediasphere—perhaps their primary affordance—is the possibility of foregrounding evidence over interpretation and overnarrativization. Whether through physical media, performance, presence, social practice, or digital technologies, new means of evidence-based cultural intervention will continue to arise. And yet I'm not sure we're well served by an excess of affordances. Look at Flaubert's Bouvard and Pécuchet, lost in the nineteenth-century supermarket of ideas, and their homebuilt laboratory filled with equipment used once to perform inconclusive experiments. Or their New England equivalent, the Peterkin family as chronicled in *The Peterkin Papers* (which I interpret as a satire on the Transcendentalists), who, in one story, go to great effort to source for their son Solomon John the paper, ink, and quills he needs for the book he so much wants to write, and then, when he sits down at his desk surrounded by family members he looks up and states, "But I haven't got anything to say!" (Hale 1868).

> "Alas! and woe is me!" thus bemoaned himself a heavy-looking gentleman in green spectacles. "The world is utterly ruined, and there is nothing to live for any longer. The business of my life is snatched from me. Not a volume to be had for love or money!" . . .

"My dear sir," said I to the desperate bookworm, "is not nature better than a book? Is not the human heart deeper than any system of philosophy? Is not life replete with more instruction than past observers have found it possible to write down in maxims? Be of good cheer. The great book of Time is still spread wide open before us; and, if we read it aright, it will be to us a volume of eternal truth."

"O, my books, my books, my precious printed books!" reiterated the forlorn bookworm.

"My only reality was a bound volume; and now they will not leave me even a shadowy pamphlet!"

In fact, the last remnant of the literature of all the ages was now descending upon the blazing heap in the shape of a cloud of pamphlets from the press of the New World. These likewise were consumed in the twinkling of an eye, leaving the earth, for the first time since the days of Cadmus, free from the plague of letters,—an enviable field for the authors of the next generation. . . .

"Well, and does anything remain to be done?" inquired I, somewhat anxiously. "Unless we set fire to the earth itself, and then leap boldly off into infinite space, I know not that we can carry reform to any farther point." (Nathaniel Hawthorne, "Earth's Holocaust")

Notes

The point of departure for this chapter is the keynote talk the author delivered at the Terms of Media II Actions conference at Brown University on October 8, 2015, but this text is heavily revised and extended.

1   @footage is the author. All textual extracts in this chapter credited to a Twitter handle are verbatim Tweets.

2   Bethany Nowviskie (2016a and b) calls for the reformulation of digital collections and digital scholarship "to fuel the conceptualization and the realization of alternative futures," invoking Afrofuturist thought and the fusion of community archival practice with speculative thinking, as exemplified in the work of Rasheedah Phillips's Community Futures Lab. (https://www.blackquantumfuturism.com/, accessed April 15, 2017.).

3   Jarrett M. Drake (2016a and b) critiques "the traditional way of doing archives," outlines the risks of reformism and describes "the transformative power of liberatory and community archives" in an essential, two-part article.

4   Michelle Caswell's essential paper (2016) describes the "failure of interdisciplinarity" between humanities scholarship and archival studies.

5   Tansey (2016) describes the "marginalization from the public sphere" that affects archivists, despite their essential role in maintaining the historical and cultural record.

6   As far as I can determine, Jessa Lingel (2016) was the first writer to explicitly link "the fetish of the archive" with the unwillingness of outsiders to recognize archival labor. Archivist Hillel Arnold (2016) suggests that maintenance studies is a framework for understanding archivists' marginalization and invisibility.

7   Greene and Meissner (2005) examined and critiqued the ritualistic nature of textual archival processing in a paper that remains controversial ten years after its publication.

8   @bspalmieri is Brooke S. Palmieri.

9   Drake (2016a) names and eloquently critiques three characteristics of traditional archives, comparing them to the carceral vision embodied in Philadelphia's Eastern State Penitentiary, opened 1829: "silence, solitude and surveillance."

10. Consideration of analogies and relationships between knowledge and information infrastructures and infrastructures of cities populates the work of scholar Shannon Mattern (2016).

11 The effects of this tragedy are still seen today in the Draconian fire codes governing storage of nitrate film (Greene and Newell 1929).

12 For years nitrate decomposition was believed to increase the danger of combustibility, until Heather Heckman's (2010) literature survey established that this relationship was based more on faith than on research..

13 A stellar assembly of archivists, scholars, and devotees have contributed to such a project: cf. Smither and Surowiec (2002).

14 For an exhaustive and well-researched survey of silent feature film survival, see Pierce 2013.

15 An entertaining compilation of studio-produced stock footage and process plates may be seen at https://archive.org/details/InternetArchive35mmStock-FootageSampleReel (accessed July 1, 2018).

16 "Poems are considered frivolous, but they have jobs to do. They offer up space to make sense of not just language, but being." Jen Bervin, speaking at the Creative Capital Artist Retreat, Williams College, 2013, at https://aroomof teresasown.wordpress.com/2014/10/14/quote-of-the-day-jen-bervin/, accessed August 25, 2016.

17 See Schiller and Prelinger 2017.

18 A visit to a nontraditional library resensitized Kevin Kelly, a longtime advocate of digitality, to books and their affordances. See Kelly 2011.

19 See Soar and Gallant 2016.

20 @john_overholt is John Overholt. @mchris4duke is Chris Bourg.

21 @snowdenbecker is Snowden Becker.

22   See Leary 2011.

23   As of mid-2018, I have produced 24 film/events of this type, which have been presented before 100 live audiences. See Schiller and Prelinger 2017.

24   Paraphrasing Erika Mijlin's remarks at the Poetics and Politics Documentary Research Symposium, U.C. Santa Cruz, May 17, 2015. Mijlin's sentiment hints at the hierarchies and moral panics linked with differing domains of collecting. The moral panics and pathologies that generally surround hoarding should not deter archivists from thinking seriously about what it can teach them. Scott Herring (2014) examines the socially devalued and highly pathologized practice of hoarding in his thoughtful and courageous book, which is also an examination of vernacular archival practice on another level and a book I highly recommend to archivists and archival scholars. Many people who are seen as hoarders (including Andy Warhol, who assembled more than six hundred of his "time capsules") may well be working toward some of the same objectives archives are organized to address. Anna Chen (2015) encourages archivists to consider "digital hoarding" and "individual organizational practices" as organic activities that may usefully inform archival practices.

25   Akin, perhaps, to the escalation in citation of the "mosaic theory" by U.S. federal agencies as grounds for exempting information from public release under the Freedom of Information Act. See Pozen 2005.

26   Scholar Kimberly Christen (2012 and 2018) has collaborated with Indigenous communities to develop archival management systems and platforms for managing their curatorial and archival needs. Critiquing generalized calls for "openness," she advocates the incorporation of "a wider range of ethical and cultural concerns into our digital tools."

27   By quoting Eichhorn as part of a discussion of amateurism, I do not mean to imply that she privileges personal and community collecting over institutional collecting. "For a generation or two of women born during and following the rise of the second wave feminist movement, inaugurating private and semipublic collections as archives and donating them to established public and university archives and collections is central to how they legitimize their voices in the public sphere" (Eichhorn 2013, 15).

28   The book contains tipped-in and glued-in photographs, microfilm and microprint samples, printing plates, mimeographed sheets and newsprint, all of which resist conventional mass-digitization processes. See Binkley 1936.

29   @ncecire is Natalia Cecire.

References

Arnold, Hillel. 2016. "Critical Work: Archivists as Maintainers," *hillelarnold.com*. Accessed August 16, 2016. http://hillelarnold.com/blog/2016/08/critical-work/.

Bervin, Jen. 2013. "Remarks at the Creative Capital Artist Retreat, Williams College." Accessed August 25, 2016. https://aroomofteresasown.wordpress.com/2014/10/14/quote-of-the-day-jen-bervin/.

Binkley, Peter (initial contributor). 2016. Initially created March 17, 2013. Accessed August 28, 2016. https://en.wikipedia.org/wiki/Robert_C._Binkley. Article written largely by Binkley's grandson and contemporary explicator Peter Binkley, which describes Binkley's writing on decentralized and amateur scholarship and links to major writings.

Binkley, Robert C. 1936. *Manual on Methods of Reproducing Research Materials: A Survey Made for the Joint Committee on Materials for Research of the Social Science Research Council and the American Council of Learned Societies.* Ann Arbor, Mich.: Edwards Brothers.

Bornholt, James, Randolph Lopez, Douglas M. Carmean, Luis Ceze, Georg Seelig, and Karin Strauss. 2016. "A DNA-Based Archival Storage System." In *International Conference on Architectural Support for Programming Languages and Operating Systems.* Accessed June 25, 2016. https://homes.cs.washington.edu/~luisceze/publications/dnastorage-asplos16.pdf.

Brooks, Van Wyck. 1961. *From the Shadow of the Mountain: My Post-Meridian Years.* New York: E. P. Dutton.

Caswell, Michelle. 2016. "'The Archive' Is Not An Archives: Acknowledging the Intellectual Contributions of Archival Studies," *Reconstruction* 16, no. 1. Accessed June 28, 2016. http://reconstruction.eserver.org/Issues/161/Caswell.shtml.

Chen, Anna. 2014. "Disorder: Vocabularies of Hoarding in Personal Digital Archiving Practices," *Archivaria* 78 (Fall): 115–34.

Christen, Kimberly. 2012. "Does Information Really Want to Be Free? Indigenous Knowledge Systems and the Question of Openness." *International Journal of Communication* 6, 2870–93. Accessed July 1, 2018. http://www.kimchristen.com/wp-content/uploads/2015/07/christen6.2012.pdf.

Christen, Kimberly. 2018. "Publications." Accessed July 1, 2018. https://www.kim christen.com/publications/.

Darms, Lisa. 2015. Introduction to "Radical Archives" section of "Archives Remixed" issue, *Archive Journal* 5 (Fall). Accessed June 24, 2016. http://www.archivejournal .net/issue/5/archives-remixed/.

Drake, Jarrett M. 2016a. "Liberatory Archives: Towards Belonging and Believing (Part 1)." Delivered at the first Community Archives Forum at UCLA on October 21, 2016. *medium.com.* Accessed April 15, 2017. https://medium.com/on-archivy/liberatory-archives-towards-belonging-and-believing-part-1-d26aaeb0edd1.

Drake, Jarrett M. 2016b. "Liberatory Archives: Towards Belonging and Believing (Part 2)." Delivered at the first Community Archives Forum at UCLA on October 21, 2016. *medium.com.* Accessed April 15, 2017. https://medium.com/on-archivy/liberatory-archives-towards-belonging-and-believing-part-2-6f56c754eb17.

Eichhorn, Kate. 2013. *The Archival Turn in Feminism: Outrage in Order.* Philadelphia: Temple University Press.

Greene, F. E., and H. E. Newell. 1929. *Report on the Cleveland Clinic Fire, Cleveland, Ohio, May 15, 1929, by the National Board of Fire Underwriters and the Ohio Inspection Bureau.* New York: National Board of Fire Underwriters. Accessed August 25, 2016. http://cplorg.cdmhost.com/cdm/ref/collection/p128201coll0/id/3512.

Greene, Mark A., and Dennis Meissner. 2005. "More Product, Less Process:

Revamping Traditional Archival Processing." *American Archivist* 68: 208–63. Accessed June 20, 2016. http://www.archivists.org/prof-education/pre-readings/IMPLP/AA68.2.MeissnerGreene.pdf.

Hale, Lucretia P. 1868. "The Peterkins Try to Become Wise." *Our Young Folks* 4 (May), 270–71. *books.google.com.* Accessed August 29, 2016. https://books.google.com/books?id=GyzyAAAAMAAJ&lpg=PA270&ots=5IuxlEnDz-&dq=peterkins%20try%20to%20become%20wise&pg=PA271#v=onepage&q=peterkins%20try%20to%20become%20wise&f=false.

Hawthorne, Nathaniel. 1844. "Earth's Holocaust." In *Mosses from an Old Manse. eldritchpress.org.* Accessed June 25, 2016. http://www.eldritchpress.org/nh/holo.html.

Heckman, Heather. 2010. "Burn after Viewing, or Fire in the Vaults: Nitrate Decomposition and Combustibility," *American Archivist* 73, no. 2: 483–506.

Herring, Scott. 2014. *The Hoarders: Material Deviance in Modern American Culture.* Chicago: University of Chicago Press.

Jardine, Boris, and Christopher Kelty. 2016. "Preface: The Total Archive," *Limn* 6 (March). Accessed August 25, 2016. http://limn.it/preface-the-total-archive/.

Kelly, Kevin. 2011. "The Gravity of Paper." *The Technium* (April 11). Accessed June 24, 2016. http://kk.org/thetechnium/the-gravity-of/.

Leary, John Patrick. 2011. "Detroitism," *Guernica* (January 15). Accessed June 20, 2016. https://www.guernicamag.com/features/leary_1_15_11/.

Lingel, Jessa. 2013. "This Is Not an Archive," *jessalingel.tumblr.com.* November 5. Accessed June 25, 2016. http://jessalingel.tumblr.com/post/66108958850/this-is-not-an-archive.

Mariano, Paul, and Kurt Norton. 2011. *These Amazing Shadows* (film). Gravitas Docufilms. http://www.imdb.com/title/tt1273222/

Mattern, Shannon. 2016. *wordsinspace.net.* Accessed June 20, 2016. http://www.wordsinspace.net.

Mueller, Pam A., and Daniel M. Oppenheimer. 2014. "The Pen Is Mightier than the Keyboard: Advantages of Longhand over Laptop Note Taking." *Psychological Science* 25, no. 6: 1159–68. Accessed August 17, 2016. http://pss.sagepub.com/content/25/6/1159.full?keytype=ref&siteid=sppss&ijkey=CjRAwmrIURGNw.

Nowviskie, Bethany, 2016a. "alternate futures/usable pasts," *nowviskie.org.* October 24, 2016. Accessed April 15, 2017. http://nowviskie.org/2016/alternate-futures-usable-pasts/.

Nowviskie, Bethany, 2016b. "speculative collections," *nowviskie.org.* October 27, 2016. Accessed April 15, 2017. http://nowviskie.org/2016/speculative-collections/.

Pierce, David. 2013. *The Survival of American Silent Feature Films: 1912–1929,* Washington, D.C.: Council on Library and Information Resources and Library of Congress. Accessed August 25, 2016. https://www.loc.gov/programs/static/national-film-preservation-board/documents/pub158.final_version_sept_2013.pdf.

Pozen, David E. 2005. "The Mosaic Theory, National Security, and the Freedom of Information Act," *Yale Law Journal* 115, no. 3: 628–78. Accessed August 25, 2016. http://www.yalelawjournal.org/note/the-mosaic-theory-national-security-and-the-freedom-of-information-act.

Prelinger, Rick. 2009. "Taking History Back from the 'Storytellers.'" *blackoystercatcher .blogspot.com.* Accessed June 20, 2016. http://blackoystercatcher.blogspot.com /2009/06/taking-history-back-from-storytellers.html.

Prelinger, Rick. 2010. "We Are the New Archivists: Artisans, Activists, Cinephiles, Citizens." Talk presented at "Reimagining the Archive" Symposium, UCLA, November 12, 2010. Accessed July 1, 2018. https://www.slideshare.net/footage/ reimagining-the-archive-keynote-presentation.

Prelinger, Rick. 2015. "The Disappearance of Archives." In Wendy Hui Kyong Chun, Anna Watkins Fisher, and Thomas Keenan, *New Media, Old Media: A History and Theory Reader,* 2nd Edition. New York: Routledge, 2015.

Prelinger, Rick, and Internet Archive. 2000. "Prelinger Collection." Website that originated December 30, 2000. Accessed June 25, 2016. http://www.archive.org/ details/prelinger.

Prelinger, Rick, and Megan Prelinger. 2018. "Prelinger Library." Accessed July 1, 2018. http://prelingerlibrary.org.

Schiller, Lucy, and Rick Prelinger. 2017. "Essayistic Interventions: Taking the City into the Theater." *The Essay Review* (Iowa City). Accessed July 1, 2018. http://theessay review.org/essayistic-interventions-taking-the-city-into-the-theater/

Slide, Anthony. 1992. *Nitrate Won't Wait: A History of Film Preservation in the United States,* Jefferson, N.C.: McFarland.

Smither, Roger, and Catherine A. Surowiec, eds. 2002. *This Film Is Dangerous: A Celebration of Nitrate Film.* Brussels: International Federation of Film Archives.

Soar, Matt, and Jackie Gallant. 2016. "Lost Leaders: Countdowns and the Metadata of Film (2011–)." *lostleaders.ca.* Accessed June 24, 2016. www.lostleaders.ca.

Tansey, Eira. 2016. "Archives without Archivists," *Reconstruction* 16, no. 1. Accessed June 28, 2016. http://reconstruction.eserver.org/Issues/161/Tansey.shtml.

Wizisla, Erdmut, Helgrid Streidt, Heidrun Loeper, and Bertolt-Brecht-Archiv, Akademie der Künste. 2007. *Die Bibliothek Bertolt Brechts.* Frankfurt am Main: Suhrkamp Verlag.

System of a Takedown: Control and De-commodification in the Circuits of Academic Publishing

Marcell Mars and Tomislav Medak

Since 2012 the Public Library/Memory of the World[1] project has been developing and publicly supporting scenarios for massive disobedience against the current regulation of production and circulation of knowledge and culture in the digital realm. While the significance of that year may not be immediately apparent to everyone, across the peripheries of an unevenly developed world of higher education and research it produced a resonating void. The takedown of the book-sharing site Library.nu in early 2012 gave rise to an anxiety that the equalizing effect that its piracy had created—the fact that access to the most recent and relevant scholarship was no longer a privilege of rich academic institutions in a few countries of the world (or, for that matter, the exclusive preserve of academia to begin with)—would simply disappear into thin air. While alternatives within these peripheries quickly filled the gap, it was only through an unlikely set of circumstances that they were able to do so, let alone continue to exist in light of the legal persecution they now also face.

The starting point for the Public Library/Memory of the World project was a simple consideration: the public library is the institutional form that societies have devised in order to make knowledge and culture accessible to all their members regardless of social or economic status. There's a political consensus that this principle of access is fundamental to the purpose of a modern society. Yet, as digital networks have radically expanded the access to literature and scientific research, public libraries were largely denied the ability to extend to digital "objects" the kind of de-commodified access they provide in the world of print. For instance, libraries frequently don't have the right to purchase e-books for lending and preservation. If they do, they are limited by how many times— twenty-six in the case of one publisher—and under what conditions they can lend them before not only the license but the "object" itself is revoked. In the case of academic journals, it is even worse: as they move to predominantly digital models of distribution, libraries can provide access to and "preserve" them only for as long as they pay extortionate prices for ongoing subscriptions. By building tools for organizing and sharing electronic libraries, creating digitization workflows, and making books available online, the Public Library/Memory of the World project is aimed at helping to fill the space that remains denied to real-world public libraries. It is obviously not alone in this effort. There are many other platforms, some more public, some more secretive, working to help people share books. And the practice of sharing is massive.

—https://www.memoryoftheworld.org

Capitalism and Schizophrenia

New media remediate old media. Media pay homage to their (mediatic) predecessors, which themselves pay homage to their own (mediatic) predecessors. Computer graphics remediate film, which remediates photography, which remediates painting, and so on (McLuhan 1965, 8; Bolter and Grusin 1999). Attempts to understand new media technologies always settle on a set of metaphors (of the old and familiar), in order to approximate what is similar, and yet at the same time name the new. Every such metaphor has its semiotic distance, decay, or inverse-square law that draws the limit how far the metaphor can go in its explanation of the phenomenon to which it is applied. The intellectual work in the Age of Mechanical Reproduction thus received an unfortunate metaphor: intellectual property. A metaphor modeled on the scarce and exclusive character of property over land. As the Age of Mechanical Reproduction became more and more the Age of Discrete and Digital Reproduction, another metaphor emerged, one that reveals the quandary left after decades of decay resulting from the increasing distanciation of intellectual property from the intellectual work it seeks to regulate, and that metaphor is: schizophrenia.

Technologies compete with each other—the discrete and the digital thus competes with the mechanical—and the aftermath of these clashes can be dramatic. People lose their jobs, companies go bankrupt, disciplines lose their departments, and computer users lose their old files. More often than not, clashes between competing technologies create antagonisms between different social groups. Their voices are (sometimes) heard, and society tries to balance their interests.

If the institutional remedies cannot resolve the social antagonism, the law is called on to mediate. Yet in the present, the legal system only reproduces the schizoid impasse where the metaphor of property over land is applied to works of intellect that have in practical terms become universally accessible in the digital world. Court cases do not result in a restoration of balance but rather in the confirmation of entrenched interests. It is, however, not necessary that courts act in such a one-sided manner. As Cornelia Vismann (2011) reminds us in her analysis of the ancient roots of legal mediation, the juridical process has two facets: first, a theatrical aspect that has common roots with the Greek dramatic theatre and its social function as a translator of a *matter* of conflict into a *case* for weighted juridical debate; second, an agonistic aspect not unlike a sporting competition where a winner has to be decided, one that leads to judgment and sanction. In the matter of copyright versus access, however, the fact that courts cannot look past the metaphor of intellectual property, which reduces any understanding of our contemporary technosocial condition to an analogy with the scarcity-based language of property over land, has meant that they have failed to adjudicate a matter of conflict between the equalizing effects of universal access to knowledge and the guarantees of rightful remuneration for intellectual labor into a meaningful social resolution. Rather they have primarily reasserted the agonistic aspect by supporting exclusively the commercial interests of large copyright industries that structure and deepen that conflict at the societal level.

This is not surprising. As many other elements of contemporary law, the legal norms of copyright were articulated and codified through the centuries-long development of the capitalist state and world-system. The legal system is, as Nicos Poulantzas (2008, 25–26) suggests, genetically structured by capitalist development. And yet at the same time it is semi-autonomous; the development of its norms and institutional aspects is largely endogenous and partly responsive to the specific needs of other social subsystems. Still, if the law and the courts are the codified and lived rationality of a social formation, then the choice of intellectual property as a metaphor in capitalist society comes as no surprise, as its principal objective is to institute a formal political-economic framework for the commodification of intellectual labor that produces knowledge and culture. There can be no balance, only subsumption and accumulation. Capitalism and schizophrenia.

Schizophrenia abounds wherever the discrete and the digital breaking barriers to access meets capitalism. One can only wonder how the conflicting interests of different divisions get disputed and negotiated in successful corporate giants like Sony Group where Sony Pictures Entertainment,[2] Sony Music Entertainment[3] and Sony Computer Entertainment coexist under the same roof with the Sony Electronics division, which invented the Walkman back in 1979 and went on to manufacture devices and gadgets like

home (and professional) audio and video players/recorders (VHS,
Betamax, TV, HiFi, cassette, CD/DVD, mp3, mobile phones, etc.),
storage devices, personal computers, and game consoles. In the
famous 1984 Betamax case ("Sony Corp. of America v. Universal
City Studios, Inc.," Wikipedia 2015), Universal Studios and the Walt
Disney Company sued Sony for aiding copyright infringement with
their Betamax video recorders. Sony won. The court decision in
favor of fair use rather than copyright infringement laid the legal
ground for home recording technology as the foundation of future
analog, and subsequently digital, content sharing.

Five years later, Sony bought its first major Hollywood studio:
Columbia Pictures. In 2004 Sony Music Entertainment merged with
Bertelsmann Music Group to create Sony BMG. However, things
changed as Sony became the content producer and we entered the
age of the discrete and the digital. Another five years later, in 2009,
Sony BMG sued Joel Tenenbaum for downloading and then sharing
thirty-one songs. The jury awarded US$675,000 to the music
companies (US$22,000 per song). This is known as "the second
file-sharing case." "The first file-sharing case" was 2007's Capitol Records, Inc. v. Thomas-Rasset, which concerned the downloading of
twenty-four songs. In the second file-sharing case, the jury awarded
music companies US$1,920,000 in statutory damages (US$80,000
per song). The defendant, Jammie Thomas, was a Native American
mother of four from Brainerd, Minnesota, who worked at the time
as a natural resources coordinator for the Mille Lacs Band of the
Native American Ojibwe people. The conflict between access and
copyright took a clear social relief.

Encouraged by the court decisions in the years that followed, the
movie and music industries have started to publicly claim staggering numbers in annual losses: US$58 billion and 370,000 lost jobs
in the United States alone. The purported losses in sales were,
however, at least seven times bigger than the actual losses and,
if the jobs figures had been true, after only one year there would
have been no one left working in the content industry (Reid 2012).
Capitalism and schizophrenia.

If there is a reason to make an exception from the landed logic of property being imposed onto the world of the intellect, a reason to which few would object, it would be for access for educational purposes. Universities in particular give an institutional form to the premise that equal access to knowledge is a prerequisite for building a society where all people are equal.

In this noble endeavor to make universal access to knowledge central to social development, some universities stand out more than the others. Consider, for example, the Massachusetts Institute of Technology (MIT). The Free Culture and Open Access movements have never hidden their origins, inspiration, and model in the success of the Free Software Movement, which was founded in 1984 by Richard Stallman while he was working at the MIT Artificial Intelligence lab. It was at the MIT Museum that the "Hall of Hacks" was set up to proudly display the roots of hacking culture. Hacking culture at MIT takes many shapes and forms. MIT hackers famously put a fire truck (2006) and a campus police car (1994) onto the roof of the Great Dome of the campus's Building 10; they landed (and then exploded) a weather balloon onto the pitch of Harvard Stadium during a Harvard–Yale football game; turned the quote that "getting an education from MIT is like taking a drink from a Fire Hose" into a literal fire hydrant serving as a drinking fountain in front of the largest lecture hall on campus; and many, many other "hacks" (Peterson 2011).

The World Wide Web Consortium was founded at MIT in 1993. Presently its mission states as its goal "to enable human communication, commerce, and opportunities to share knowledge," on the principles of "Web for All" and the corresponding, more technologically focused "Web on Everything." Similarly, MIT began its OpenCourseWare project in 2002 in order "to publish all of [MIT's] course materials online and make them widely available to everyone" (n.d.). The One Laptop Per Child project was created in 2005 in order to help children "learn, share, create, and collaborate" (2010). Recently the MIT Media Lab (2017) has even started its own Disobedience Award, which "will go to a living person or group engaged in what we believe is extraordinary disobedience for the benefit of society . . . seeking both expected and unexpected nominees." When it comes to the governance of access to MIT's own resources, it is well known that anyone who is registered and connected to the "open campus" wireless network, either by being physically present or via VPN, can search JSTOR, Google Scholar, and other databases in order to access otherwise paywalled journals from major publishers such as Reed Elsevier, Wiley-Blackwell, Springer, Taylor and Francis, or Sage.

The MIT Press has also published numerous books that we love and without which we would have never developed the Public Library/Memory of the World project to the stage where it is now. For instance, only after reading Markus Krajewski's *Paper Machines: About Cards & Catalogs, 1548–1929* (2011) and learning how conceptually close librarians came to the universal Turing machine with the invention of the index card catalog did we center the Public Library/Memory of the World around the idea of the catalog. Eric von Hippel's *Democratizing Innovation* (2005) taught us how end users could become empowered to innovate and accordingly we have built our public library as a distributed network of amateur librarians acting as peers sharing their catalogs and books. Sven Spieker's *The Big Archive: Art from Bureaucracy* (2008) showed us the exciting hybrid meta-space between psychoanalysis, media theory, and conceptual art one could encounter by visiting the world of catalogs and archives. Understanding capitalism and schizophrenia would have been hard without Semiotext(e)'s translations of Deleuze and Guattari, and remaining on the utopian path would have been impossible if not for our reading of *Cybernetic Revolutionaries* (Medina 2011), *Imagine No Possessions* (Kiaer 2005), or *Art Power* (Groys 2008).

Our Road into Schizophrenia, Commodity Paradox, Political Strategy

Our vision for the Public Library/Memory of the World resonated with many people. After the project initially gained a large number of users, and was presented in numerous prominent artistic venues such as Museum Reina Sofía, Transmediale, Württembergischer Kunstverein, Calvert22, 98weeks, and many more, it was no small honor when Eric Kluitenberg and David Garcia invited us to write about the project for an anthology on tactical media that was to be published by the MIT Press. Tactical media is exactly where we would situate ourselves on the map. Building on Michel de Certeau's concept of tactics as agency of the weak operating in the terrain of strategic power, the tactical media (Tactical Media Files 2017) emerged in the political and technological conjuncture of the 1990s. Falling into the "art-into-life" lineage of historic avant-gardes, Situationism, DIY culture, techno-hippiedom, and media piracy, it constituted a heterogeneous field of practices and a manifestly international movement that combined experimental media and political activism into interventions that contested the post–Cold War world of global capitalism and preemptive warfare on a hybrid terrain of media, institutions, and mass movements. Practices of tactical media ranged from ephemeral media pranks, hoaxes, and hacktivism to reappropriations of media apparatuses, institutional settings, and political venues. We see our work as following in that lineage of recuperation of the means of communication from their capture by personal and impersonal structures of political or economic power.

Yet the contract for our contribution that the MIT Press sent us in early 2015 was an instant reminder of the current state of affairs in academic publishing: in return for our contribution and transfer of our copyrights, we would receive no compensation: no right to wage and no right to further distribute our work.

Only weeks later our work would land us fully into schizophrenia: the Public Library/Memory of the World received two takedown notices from the MIT Press for books that could be found in its back then relatively small yet easily discoverable online collection located at https://library.memoryoftheworld.org, including a notice for one of the books that had served as an inspiration to us: *Art Power*. First, no wage and, now, no access. A true paradox of the present-day system of knowledge production: products of our labor are commodities, yet the labor-power producing them is denied the same status. While the project's vision resonates with many, including the MIT Press, it has to be shut down. Capitalism and schizophrenia.[4]

Or, maybe, not. Maybe we don't have to go down that impasse. Starting from the two structural circumstances imposed on us by the MIT Press—the denial of wage and the denial of access—we can begin to analyze why copyright infringement is not merely, as the industry and the courts would have it, a matter of illegality. But rather a matter of legitimate action.

Over the past three decades a deep transformation, induced by the factors of technological change and economic restructuring, has been unfolding at different scales, changing the way works of culture and knowledge are produced and distributed across an unevenly developed world. As new technologies are adopted, generalized, and adapted to the realities of the accumulation process—a process we could see unfolding with the commodification of the internet over the past fifteen years—the core and the periphery adopt different strategies of opposition to the inequalities and exclusions these technologies start to reproduce. The core, with its emancipatory and countercultural narratives, pursues strategies that develop legal, economic, or technological alternatives. However, these strategies frequently fail to secure broader transformative effects as the competitive forces of the market appropriate, marginalize, or make obsolete the alternatives they advocate. Such seems to have been the destiny of much of the free software, open access, and free culture alternatives that have developed over this period.

In contrast, the periphery, in order to advance, relies on strategies of "stealing" that bypass socioeconomic barriers by refusing to submit to the harmonized regulation that sets the frame for global economic exchange. The piracy of intellectual property or industrial secrets thus creates a shadow system of exchange resisting the asymmetries of development in the world economy. However, its illegality serves as a pretext for the governments and companies of the core to devise and impose further controls over the techno-social systems that facilitate these exchanges.

Both strategies develop specific politics—a politics of reform, on the one hand, and a politics of obfuscation and resistance, on the other—yet both are defensive politics that affirm the limitations of what remains inside and what remains outside of the politically legitimate.

The copyright industry giants of the past and the IT industry giants of the present are thus currently sorting it out to whose greater benefit will this new round of commodification work out. For those who find themselves outside of the the camps of these two factions of capital, there's a window of opportunity, however, to reconceive the mode of production of literature and science that has been with us since the beginning of the print trade and the dawn of capitalism. It's a matter of change, at the tail end of which ultimately lies a dilemma: whether we're going to live in a more equal or a more unjust, a more commonised or a more commodified world.

Authorship, Law, and Legitimacy

Before we can talk of such structural transformation, the normative question we expect to be asked is whether something that is considered a matter of law and juridical decision can be made a matter of politics and political process. Let's see.

Copyright has a fundamentally economic function—to unambiguously establish individualized property in the products of creative labor. A clear indication of this economic function is the substantive requirement of originality that the work is expected to have in order to be copyrightable. Legal interpretations set a very low standard on what counts as original, as their function is no more than to demarcate one creative contribution from another. Once a legal title is unambiguously assigned, there is a person holding property with whose consent the contracting, commodification, and marketing of the work can proceed.[5] In that respect copyright is not that different from the requirement of formal freedom that is granted to a laborer to contract out their own labor-power as a commodity to capital, giving capital authorization to extract maximum productivity and appropriate the products of the laborer's labor.[6] Copyright might be just a more efficient mechanism of exploitation as it unfolds through selling of produced commodities and not labor power. Art market obscures and mediates the capital-labor relation

When we talk today of illegal copying, we primarily mean an infringement of the legal rights of authors and publishers. There's an immediate assumption that the infringing practice of illegal copying and distribution falls under the domain of juridical sanction, that it is a matter of law. Yet if we look to the history of copyright, the illegality of copying was a political matter long before it became a legal one.

Publisher's rights, author's rights, and mechanisms of reputation—the three elements that are fundamental to the present-day copyright system—all have their historic roots in the context of absolutism and early capitalism in seventeenth- and eighteenth-century Europe. Before publishers and authors were given a temporary monopoly over the exploitation of their publications instituted in the form of copyright, they were operating in a system where they were forced to obtain a privilege to print books from royal censors. The first printing privileges granted to publishers, in early seventeenth-century Great Britain,[7] came with the responsibility of publishers to control what was being published and disseminated in a growing body of printed matter that started to reach the public in the aftermath of the invention of print and the rise of the reading culture. The illegality in these early days of print referred either to printing books without the permission of the censor or printing books that were already published by another printer in the territory where the censor held authority. The transition from the privilege tied to the publisher to the privilege tied to the natural person of the author would unfold only later.

In the United Kingdom this transition occurred as the guild of printers, Stationers' Company, failed to secure the extension of its printing monopoly and thus, in order to continue with its business, decided to advocate the introduction of copyright for the authors instead. This resulted in the passing of the Copyright Act of 1709, also known as the Statute of Anne (Rose 2010). The censoring authority and enterprising publishers now proceeded in lockstep to isolate the author as the central figure in the regulation of literary and scientific production. Not only did the author receive exclusive rights to the work, the author was also made—as Foucault has famously analyzed (Foucault 1980, 124)—the identifiable subject of scrutiny, censorship, and political sanction by the absolutist state.

Although the Romantic author slowly took the center stage in copyright regulations, economic compensation for the work would long remain no more than honorary. Until well into the eighteenth century, literary writing and creativity in general were regarded as resulting from divine inspiration and not the individual genius of the author. Writing was a work of honor and distinction, not something requiring an honest day's pay.[8] Money earned in the growing printing industry mostly stayed in the pockets of publishers, while the author received literally an honorarium, a flat sum that served as a "token of esteem" (Woodmansee 1996, 42). It is only once authors began to voice demands for securing their material and political independence from patronage and authority that they also started to make claims for rightful remuneration.

Thus, before it was made a matter of law, copyright was a matter of politics and economy.

Copyright, Labor, and Economic Domination

The full-blown affirmation of the Romantic author-function marks the historic moment where a compromise is established between the right of publishers to the economic exploitation of works and the right of authors to rightful compensation for those works. Economically, this redistribution from publishers to authors was made

possible by the expanding market for printed books in the eighteenth and nineteenth centuries, while politically this was catalyzed
by the growing desire for the autonomy of scientific and literary
production from the system of feudal patronage and censorship
in gradually liberalizing and modernizing capitalist societies. The
newfound autonomy of production was substantially coupled to
production specifically for the market. However, this irenic balance
could not last for very long. Once the production of culture and
science was subsumed under the exigencies of the generalized
market, it had to follow the laws of commodification and competition from which no form of commodity production can escape.

By the beginning of the twentieth century, copyright expanded to
a number of other forms of creativity, transcending its primarily
literary and scientific ambit and becoming part of the broader
set of intellectual property rights that are fundamental to the
functioning and positioning of capitalist enterprise. The corpora-
tization of the production of culture and knowledge thus brought
about a decisive break from the Romantic model that singularized
authorship in the person of the author. The production of cultural
commodities nowadays involves a number of creative inputs from
both credited (but mostly unwaged) and uncredited (but mostly
waged) contributors. The "moral rights of the author," a substantive
link between the work and the person of the author, are markedly
out of step with these realities, yet they still perform an important
function in the moral economy of reputation, which then serves as
the legitimation of copyright enforcement and monopoly. Moral
rights allow easy attribution; incentivize authors to subsidize
publishers by self-financing their own work in the hope of topping
the sales charts, rankings, or indexes; and help markets develop
along winner-takes-all principles.

The level of concentration in industries primarily concerned with
various forms of intellectual property rights is staggering. The film
industry is a US$88 billion industry dominated by six major studios
(PwC 2015c). The recorded music industry is an almost US$20
billion industry dominated by only three major labels (PwC 2015b).

The publishing industry is a US$120 billion industry where the leading ten companies earn in revenues more than the next forty largest publishing groups (PwC 2015a; Wischenbart 2014).

The Oligopoly and Academic Publishing

Academic publishing in particular draws the state of play into stark relief. It's a US$10 billion industry dominated by five publishers and financed up to 75 percent from library subscriptions. It's notorious for achieving extreme year-on-year profit margins—in the case of Reed Elsevier regularly over 30 percent, with Taylor and Francis, Springer, Wiley-Blackwell and Sage barely lagging behind (Larivière, Haustein, and Mongeon 2015). Given that the work of contributing authors is not paid but rather financed by their institutions (provided, that is, that they are employed at an institution) and that these publications nowadays come mostly in the form of electronic articles licensed under subscription for temporary use to libraries and no longer sold as printed copies, the public interest could be served at a much lower cost by leaving commercial closed-access publishers out of the equation entirely.

But that cannot be done, of course. The chief reason for this is that the system of academic reputation and ranking based on publish-or-perish principles is historically entangled with the business of academic publishers. Anyone who doesn't want to put their academic career at risk is advised to steer away from being perceived as reneging on that not-so-tacit deal. While this is patently clear to many in academia, opting for the alternative of open access means not playing by the rules, and not playing by the rules can have real-life consequences, particularly for younger academics. Early career scholars have to publish in prestigious journals if they want to advance in the highly competitive and exclusive system of academia (Kendzior 2012).

Copyright in academic publishing has thus become simply a mechanism of the direct transfer of economic power from producers to publishers, giving publishers an instrument for maintaining their stranglehold on the output of academia. But publishers also have control over metrics and citation indexes, pandering to the authors with better tools for maximizing their impact and self-promotion. Reputation and copyright are extortive instruments that publishers can wield against authors and the public to prevent an alternative from emerging.[9]

The state of the academic publishing business signals how the "copyright industries" in general might continue to control the field as their distribution model now transitions to streaming or licensed-access models. In the age of cloud computing, autonomous infrastructures run by communities of enthusiasts are becoming increasingly a thing of the past. "Copyright industries," supported by the complicit legal system, now can pressure proxies for these infrastructures, such as providers of server colocation, virtual hosting, and domain-name network services, to enforce injunctions for them without ever getting involved in direct, costly infringement litigation. Efficient shutdowns of precarious shadow systems allow for a corporate market consolidation wherein the majority of streaming infrastructures end up under the control of a few corporations.

Illegal Yet Justified, Collective Civil Disobedience, Politicizing the Legal

However, when companies do resort to litigation or get involved in criminal proceedings, they can rest assured that the prosecution and judicial system will uphold their interests over the right of public to access culture and knowledge, even when the irrationality of the copyright system lies in plain sight, as it does in the case of academic publishing. Let's look at two examples:

On January 6, 2011, Aaron Swartz, a prominent programmer and hacktivist, was arrested by the MIT campus police and U.S. Secret Service on charges of having downloaded a large number of academic articles from the JSTOR repository. While JSTOR, with whom Swartz reached a settlement and to whom he returned the files, and, later, MIT, would eventually drop the charges, the federal prosecution decided nonetheless to indict Swartz on thirteen criminal counts, potentially leading to fifty years in prison and a US$1 million fine. Under growing pressure by the prosecution Swartz committed suicide on January 11, 2013.

Given his draconian treatment at the hands of the prosecution and the absence of institutions of science and culture that would stand up and justify his act on political grounds, much of Swartz's defense focused on trying to exculpate his acts, to make them less infringing or less illegal than the charges brought against him had claimed, a rational course of action in irrational circumstances. However, this was unfortunately becoming an uphill battle as the prosecution's attention was accidentally drawn to a statement written by Swartz in 2008 wherein he laid bare the dysfunctionality of the academic publishing system. In his *Guerrilla Open Access Manifesto,* he wrote: "The world's entire scientific and cultural heritage, published over centuries in books and journals, is increasingly being digitized and locked up by a handful of private corporations. . . . Forcing academics to pay money to read the work of their colleagues? Scanning entire libraries but only allowing the folks at Google to read them? Providing scientific articles to those at elite universities in the First World, but not to children in the Global South? It's outrageous and unacceptable." After a no-nonsense diagnosis followed an even more clear call to action: "We need to download scientific journals and upload them to file sharing networks. We need to fight for Guerilla Open Access" (Swartz 2008). Where a system has failed to change unjust laws, Swartz felt, the responsibility was on those who had access to make injustice a thing of the past.

Whether Swartz's intent actually was to release the JSTOR repository remains subject to speculation. The prosecution has never proven that it was. In the context of the legal process, his call to action was simply taken as a matter of law and not for what it was—a matter of politics. Yet, while his political action was preempted, others have continued pursuing his vision by committing small acts of illegality on a massive scale. In June 2015 Elsevier won an injunction against Library Genesis, the largest illegal repository of electronic books, journals, and articles on the Web, and its subsidiary platform for accessing academic journals, Sci-hub. A voluntary and noncommercial project of anonymous scientists mostly from Eastern Europe, Sci-hub provides as of end of 2015 access to more than 41 million academic articles either stored in its database or retrieved through bypassing the paywalls of academic publishers. The only person explicitly named in Elsevier's lawsuit was Sci-hub's founder Alexandra Elbakyan, who minced no words: "When I was working on my research project, I found out that all research papers I needed for work were paywalled. I was a student in Kazakhstan at the time and our university was not subscribed to anything" (Ernesto 2015). Being a computer scientist, she found the tools and services on the internet that allowed her to bypass the paywalls. At first, she would make articles available on internet forums where people would file requests for the articles they needed, but eventually she automated the process, making access available to everyone on the open web. "Thanks to Elsevier's lawsuit, I got past the point of no return. At this time I either have to prove we have the full right to do this or risk being executed like other 'pirates' . . . If Elsevier manages to shut down our projects or force them into the darknet, that will demonstrate an important idea: that the public does not have the right to knowledge. . . . Everyone should have access to knowledge regardless of their income or affiliation. And that's absolutely legal. Also the idea that knowledge can be a private property of some commercial company sounds absolutely weird to me" (Ernesto 2015).

If the issue of infringement is to become political, a critical mass of infringing activity has to be achieved, access technologically organized, and civil disobedience collectively manifested. Only in this way do the illegal acts stand a chance of being transformed into the legitimate acts.

Where Law Was, there Politics Shall Be

And thus we have made a full round back to where we started. The parallel development of liberalism, copyright, and capitalism has resulted in a system demanding that the contemporary subject act in accordance with two opposing tendencies: "more capitalist than capitalist and more proletarian than proletariat" (Deleuze and Guattari 1983, 34). Schizophrenia is, as Deleuze and Guattari argue, a condition that simultaneously embodies two disjunctive positions. Desire and blockage, flow and territory. Capitalism is the constant decoding of social blockages and territorializations aimed at liberating the production of desires and flows further and further, only to oppose them at its extreme limit. It decodes the old socius by means of private property and commodity production, privatization and abstraction, the flow of wealth and flows of workers (140). It allows contemporary subjects—including corporate entities such as the MIT Press or Sony—to embrace their contradictions and push them to their limits. But capturing them in the orbit of the self-expanding production of value, it stops them at going beyond its own limit. It is this orbit that the law sanctions in the present, recoding schizoid subjects into the inevitability of capitalism. The result is the persistence of a capitalist reality anti-thetical to common interest—commercial closed-access academic publishing—and the persistence of a hyperproletariat—an intel-lectual labor force that is too subsumed to organize and resist the reality that thrives parasitically on its social function. It's a schizoid impasse sustained by a failed metaphor.

The revolutionary events of the Paris Commune of 1871, its mere "existence" as Marx has called it,[10] a brief moment of "communal luxury" set in practice as Kristin Ross (2015) describes it, demanded that, in spite of any circumstances and reservations, one takes a side. And such is our present moment of truth.

Digital networks have expanded the potential for access and created an opening for us to transform the production of knowl-edge and culture in the contemporary world. And yet they have likewise facilitated the capacity of intellectual property industries to optimize, to cut out the cost of printing and physical distribution. Digitization is increasingly helping them to control access, expand copyright, impose technological protection measures, consolidate the means of distribution, and capture the academic valorization process.

As the potential opening for universalizing access to culture and knowledge created by digital networks is now closing, attempts at private legal reform such as Creative Commons licenses have had only a very limited effect. Attempts at institutional reform such as Open Access publishing are struggling to go beyond a niche. Piracy has mounted a truly disruptive opposition, but given the legal repression it has met with, it can become an agent of change only if it is embraced as a kind of mass civil disobedience. Where law was, there politics shall be.

Many will object to our demand to replace the law with politicization. Transitioning from politics to law was a social achievement as the despotism of political will was suppressed by legal norms guaranteeing rights and liberties for authors; this much is true. But in the face of the draconian, failed juridical rationality sustaining the schizoid impasse imposed by economic despotism, these developments hold little justification. Thus we return once more to the words of Aaron Swartz to whom we remain indebted for political inspiration and resolve: "There is no justice in following unjust laws. It's time to come into the light and, in the grand tradition of civil disobedience, declare our opposition to this private theft of public culture. . . . With enough of us, around the world, we'll not just send a strong message opposing the privatization of knowledge—we'll make it a thing of the past. Will you join us?" (Swartz 2008).

Notes

1   We initially named our project Public Library because we have developed it
     as a technosocial project from a minimal definition that defines public library
     as constituted by three elements: free access to books for every member of
     a society, a library catalog, and a librarian (Mars, Zarroug and Medak, 2015).
     However, this definition covers all public libraries and shadow libraries
     complementing the work of public libraries in providing digital access. We have
     thus decided to rename our project as Memory of the World, after our project's

initial domain name. This is a phrase coined by Henri La Fontaine, whose mention we found in Markus Krajewski's *Paper Machines* (2011). It turned out that UNESCO runs a project under the same name with the objective to preserve valuable archives for the whole of humanity. We have appropriated that objective. Given that this change has happened since we drafted the initial version of this text in 2015, we'll call our project in this text with a double name Public Library/Memory of the World.

2   Sony Pictures Entertainment became the owner of two (MGM, Columbia Pictures) out of eight Golden Age major movie studios ("Major Film Studio," Wikipedia 2015).

3   In 2012 Sony Music Entertainment is one of the Big Three majors ("Record Label," Wikipedia 2015).

4   Since this anecdote was recounted by Marcell in his opening keynote in the Terms of Media II conference at Brown University, we have received another batch of takedown notices from the MIT Press. It seemed as no small irony, because at the time the Terms of Media conference reader was rumored to be distributed by the MIT Press.

5   "In law, authorship is a point of origination of a property right which, thereafter, like other property rights, will circulate in the market, ending up in the control of the person who can exploit it most profitably. Since copyright serves paradoxically to vest authors with property only to enable them to divest that property, the author is a notion which needs only to be sustainable for an instant" (Bently 1994).

6   For more on the formal freedom of the laborer to sell his labor-power, see chapter 6 of Marx's *Capital* (1867).

7   For a more detailed account of the history of printing privilege in Great Britain, but also the emergence of peer review out of the self-censoring performed by the Royal Academy and Académie de sciences in return for the printing privilege, see Biagioli 2002.

8   The transition of authorship from honorific to professional is traced in Woodmansee 1996.

9   Not all publishers are necessarily predatory. For instance, scholar-led open-access publishers, such as those working under the banner of Radical Open Access (http://radicaloa.disruptivemedia.org) have been experimenting with alternatives to the dominant publishing models, workflows, and metrics, radicalizing the work of conventional open access, which has by now increasingly become recuperated by big for-profit publishers, who see in open access an opportunity to assume the control over the economy of data in academia. Some established academic publishers, too, have been open to experiments that go beyond mere open access and are trying to redesign how academic writing is produced, made accessible, and valorized. This essay has the good fortune of appearing as a joint publication of two such publishers: Meson Press and University of Minnesota Press.

10   "The great social measure of the Commune was its own working existence" (Marx 1871).

References

Bently, Lionel. 1994. "Copyright and the Death of the Author in Literature and Law." *The Modern Law Review* 57, no. 6: 973–86. Accessed January 2, 2018. doi:10.1111/j.1468–2230.1994.tb01989.x.

Biagioli, Mario. 2002. "From Book Censorship to Academic Peer Review." *Emergences: Journal for the Study of Media & Composite Cultures* 12, no. 1: 11–45.

Bolter, Jay David, and Richard Grusin. 1999. *Remediation: Understanding New Media.* Cambridge, Mass.: MIT Press.

Deleuze, Gilles, and Félix Guattari. 1983. *Anti-Oedipus: Capitalism and Schizophrenia.* Minneapolis: University of Minnesota Press.

Ernesto. 2015. "Sci-Hub Tears Down Academia's 'Illegal' Copyright Paywalls." *Torrent-Freak,* June 27. Accessed October 18, 2015. https://torrentfreak.com/sci-hub-tears-down-academias-illegal-copyright-paywalls-150627/.

Foucault, Michel. 1980. "What Is an Author?" In *Language, Counter-Memory, Practice: Selected Essays and Interviews,* ed. Donald F. Bouchard, 113–38. Ithaca, N.Y.: Cornell University Press.

Groys, Boris. 2008. *Art Power.* Cambridge, Mass.: MIT Press.

Kendzior, Sarah. 2012. "Academic Paywalls Mean Publish and Perish." *Al Jazeera English,* October 2. Accessed October 18, 2015. http://www.aljazeera.com/indepth/opinion/2012/10/20121017558785551.html.

Kiaer, Christina. 2005. *Imagine No Possessions: The Socialist Objects of Russian Constructivism.* Cambridge, Mass.: MIT Press.

Krajewski, Markus. 2011. *Paper Machines: About Cards & Catalogs, 1548–1929.* Cambridge, Mass.: MIT Press.

Larivière, Vincent, Stefanie Haustein, and Philippe Mongeon. 2015. "The Oligopoly of Academic Publishers in the Digital Era." *PLoS ONE* 10, no. 6. Accessed January 2, 2018. doi:10.1371/journal.pone.0127502.

Mars, Marcell, Marar Zarroug, and Tomislav Medak. 2015. "Public Library (essay)." in Public Library, ed. Marcell Mars and Tomislav Medak. Zagreb: Multimedia Institute & What, how & for Whom/WHW.

Marx, Karl. 1867. *Capital,* Vol. 1. Available at: *Marxists.org.* Accessed April 9, 2017. https://www.marxists.org/archive/marx/works/1867-c1/ch06.htm.

Marx, Karl. 1871. "The Civil War in France." Available at: *Marxists.org.* Accessed April 9, 2017. https://www.marxists.org/archive/marx/works/1871/civil-war-france/.

McLuhan, Marshall. 1965. *Understanding Media: The Extensions of Man.* New York: McGraw-Hill.

Medina, Eden. 2011. *Cybernetic Revolutionaries: Technology and Politics in Allende's Chile.* Cambridge, Mass. MIT Press.

MIT Media Lab. 2017. "MIT Media Lab Disobedience Award." Accessed 10 April 2017, https://media.mit.edu/disobedience/.

MIT OpenCourseWare. n.d. "About OCW | MIT OpenCourseWare | Free Online Course Materials." Accessed October 28, 2015. http://ocw.mit.edu/about/.

One Laptop per Child. 2010. "One Laptop per Child (OLPC): Vision." Accessed October 28, 2015. http://laptop.org/en/vision/.

Peterson, T. F., ed. 2011. *Nightwork: A History of Hacks and Pranks at MIT.* Cambridge, Mass.: MIT Press.

Poulantzas, Nicos. 2008. *The Poulantzas Reader: Marxism, Law, and the State.* London: Verso.

PwC. 2015a. "Book Publishing." Accessed October 18, 2015. http://www.pwc.com/gx /en/industries/entertainment-media/outlook/segment-insights/book-publishing .html.

PwC. 2015b. "Filmed Entertainment." Accessed October 18, 2015. http://www.pwc.com /gx/en/industries/entertainment-media/outlook/segment-insights/filmed-enter tainment.html.

PwC. 2015c. "Music: Growth Rates of Recorded and Live Music." Accessed October 18, 2015. http://www.pwc.com/gx/en/global-entertainment-media-outlook/assets/ 2015/music-key-insights-1-growth-rates-of-recorded-and-live-music.pdf.

Reid, Rob. 2012. "The Numbers behind the Copyright Math." *TED Blog,* March 20. Accessed October 28, 2015, http://blog.ted.com/the-numbers-behind-the -copyright-math/.

Rose, Mark. 2010. "The Public Sphere and the Emergence of Copyright." In *Privilege and Property, Essays on the History of Copyright,* ed. Ronan Deazley, Martin Kret-schmer, and Lionel Bently, 67–88. Open Book Publishers.

Ross, Kristin. 2015. *Communal Luxury: The Political Imaginary of the Paris Commune.* London: Verso.

Spieker, Sven. 2008. *The Big Archive: Art from Bureaucracy.* Cambridge, Mass.: MIT Press.

Swartz, Aaron. 2008. "Guerilla Open Access Manifesto." *Internet Archive.* Accessed October 18, 2015. https://archive.org/stream/GuerillaOpenAccessManifesto/ Goamjuly2008_djvu.txt.

Tactical Media Files. 2017. "The Concept of Tactical Media." Accessed May 4, 2017. http://www.tacticalmediafiles.net/articles/44999.

Vismann, Cornelia. 2011. *Medien der Rechtsprechung.* Frankfurt a.M.: S. Fischer Verlag.

von Hippel, Eric. 2005. *Democratizing Innovation.* Cambridge, Mass.: MIT Press.

Wikipedia, the Free Encyclopedia. 2015a. "Major Film Studio." Accessed January 2, 2018. https://en.wikipedia.org/w/index.php?title=Major_film_studio&oldid =686867076.

Wikipedia, the Free Encyclopedia. 2015b. "Record Label." Accessed January 2, 2018. https://en.wikipedia.org/w/index.php?title=Record_label&oldid=685380090.

Wikipedia, the Free Encyclopedia. 2015c. "Sony Corp. of America v. Universal City Studios, Inc." Accessed January 2, 2018. https://en.wikipedia.org/w/index.php? title=Sony_Corp._of_America_v._Universal_City_Studios,_Inc.&oldid=677390161.

Wischenbart, Rüdiger. 2015. "The Global Ranking of the Publishing Industry 2014." *Wischenbart.* Accessed October 18, 2015. http://www.wischenbart.com/upload/ Global-Ranking-of-the-Publishing-Industry_2014_Analysis.pdf.

Woodmansee, Martha. 1996. *The Author, Art, and the Market: Rereading the History of Aesthetics.* New York: Columbia University Press.

World Wide Web Consortium. n.d."W3C Mission." Accessed October 28, 2015. http:// www.w3.org/Consortium/mission.

Authors

Andrew Lison is assistant professor of media study at the University at Buffalo, the State University of New York. His writing has appeared in *New Formations, Science Fiction Studies,* and a number of edited volumes, including *The Global Sixties in Sound and Vision: Media, Counterculture, Revolt,* of which he is coeditor with Timothy Scott Brown. His work on the present volume was generously supported by a postdoctoral researchship in the digital humanities at The Hall Center for the Humanities, The University of Kansas.

Marcell Mars is research associate at the Centre for Postdigital Cultures at Coventry University (UK). Mars is one of the founders of Multimedia Institute/MAMA in Zagreb. His research, "Ruling Class Studies," started at the Jan van Eyck Academy, examines state-of-the-art digital innovation, adaptation, and intelligence created by corporations such as Google, Amazon, Facebook, and eBay. He is a doctoral student at Digital Cultures Research Lab at Leuphana University, writing a thesis on "Foreshadowed Libraries." Together with Tomislav Medak he founded Public Library/Memory of the World, for which he develops and maintains software infrastructure.

Tomislav Medak is a doctoral student at the Centre for Postdigital Cultures at Coventry University. He is a member of the theory and publishing team of Multimedia Institute/MAMA in Zagreb, as well as an amateur librarian for Public Library/Memory of the World and an artist in the performing arts collective BADco. His research focuses on technologies, capitalist development, and postcapitalist transition, particularly on economies of intellectual property and the unevenness of technoscience. He is the author of *The Hard Matter of Abstraction—A Guidebook to Domination by Abstraction* and *Shit Tech for A Shitty World.* Together with Marcell Mars he coedited *Public Library* and *Guerrilla Open Access.*

Rick Prelinger, professor of film and digital media at UC Santa Cruz, is an archivist, writer, and filmmaker. With Internet Archive, he built an open-access online repository of historical films begin ning in 2000, which now contains 7,000 freely reusable films. His films include the archival feature *Panorama Ephemera* (2004), which played in venues around the world, and *No More Road Trips?*, which received a Creative Capital grant in 2012. His twenty-five partici-patory urban history projects have played to many thousands of viewers in San Francisco, Detroit, Oakland, Los Angeles, New York, and elsewhere. He is a board member of Internet Archive and frequently writes and speaks on the future of archives and issues relating to archival access and futures. With Megan Prelinger, he cofounded and codirects an experimental research library located in downtown San Francisco.